GAMEDAY

40 DEVOTIONAL MESSAGES FOR SPIRITUAL GAMEDAY PREPARATION

REVEREND DR. DELAND J. MYERS SR. PH.D.

Foreword by

Head Coach Willie Simmons

authorHOUSE

AuthorHouse™
1663 Liberty Drive
Bloomington, IN 47403
www.authorhouse.com
Phone: 833-262-8899

Published by AuthorHouse 06/16/2023

ISBN: 979-8-8230-0993-5 (sc)
ISBN: 979-8-8230-0992-8 (e)

Library of Congress Control Number: 2023910997

Print information available on the last page.

DEDICATION

I dedicate this book to all of the hard-working coaches and staff who have dedicated their lives in support of the education and training of student athletes physically, mentally, and spiritually. I also dedicate this book to all student-athletes who work hard to compete in the sport that God has gifted them to play.

I also dedicate this book to my loving wife, Eveadean Morrison Myers who has been my co-laborer in my efforts to provide spiritual guidance and support to the coaches and their families, staff and players for the football teams I have been blessed and honored to work with.

ACKNOWLEDGEMENTS

I would like to first thank my Lord Jesus Christ for blessing me to write this book and The Holy Spirit that provided me knowledge and inspiration to write this book and as I claim the promise of Isaiah 55:11 that the words of this book, based on the Holy Scriptures, will not return void but go out and accomplish the Holy Will of God.

I want to thank the great coaches, athletic staff members and student athletes that I have worked with over the years that gave me the knowledge, inspiration and experience to write this book. Special thanks go out to Coach Craig Bohl, Head Coach of the Wyoming Cowboys Football Team and Chris Klieman, Head Coach of the Kansas State Wildcats, for giving me the opportunity to provide Gameday chapel messages to your teams during your time at North Dakota State University during many of your games, including NCAA Division I Championship Games. Special thanks also go out to Coach Willie Simmons, Head Coach of the Florida A&M University and Coach Eric Dooley, Head Coach of the Southern University Jaguars to serve as the Team Chaplin for your Football Teams at Prairie View A&M University and giving me the opportunity to not only give the Gameday chapel messages to your teams but also to work and provide spiritual support to your assistant coaches, staff, and student athletes who allowed me the opportunity to grow as a minister and share the gospel of our Lord and Savior Jesus Christ.

Last, and definitely not least, I want to thank the love of my life and most beautiful woman in the world, Eveadean Morrison Myers, for her undying love and support over the years that keeps me grounded and focused on what is most important in life; Jesus, love, and family.

She has been my support for the writing of this book and anything else that I have accomplished in life personally and professionally. I also want to thank my children, Corey, Latisha, and Deland II and our 7 Grandchildren (Zaria, Kiya, Javion, Brooklyn, Jaelyn, Sean, and Seth) for their continued love, support and fervent-effectual prayers.

TABLE OF CONTENTS

Acts 19: ¹⁵ And the evil spirit answered and said, "Jesus I know, and Paul I know; but who are you?" NKJV

1 Peter 5: ⁶ Therefore humble yourselves under the mighty hand of God, that He may exalt you in due time, ⁷ casting all your care upon Him, for He cares for you. ⁸ Be sober, be vigilant; because your adversary the devil walks about like a roaring lion, seeking whom he may devour. NKJV

1 Corinthians 9: ²⁴ Do you not know that those who run in a race all run, but one receives the prize? Run in such a way that you may obtain it. ²⁵ And everyone who competes for the prize is temperate in all things. Now they do it to obtain a perishable crown, but we for an imperishable crown. ²⁶ Therefore I run thus: not with uncertainty. Thus, I fight: not as one who beats the air. NKJV

Matthew 16: *13* When Jesus came into the region of Caesarea Philippi, He asked His disciples, saying, "Who do men say that I, the Son of Man, am?" *14* So they said, "Some say John the Baptist, some Elijah, and others Jeremiah or one of the prophets." *15* He said to them, "But who do you say that I am?" *16* Simon Peter answered and said, "You are the Christ, the Son of the living God." NKJV

Genesis 4: *6* So the LORD said to Cain, "Why are you angry? And why has your countenance fallen? *7* If you do well, will you not be accepted? And if you do not do well, sin lies at the door. And its desire is for you, but you should rule over it." NKJV

Exodus 16: *4* Then the LORD said to Moses, "Behold, I will rain bread from heaven for you. And the people shall go out and gather a certain quota every day, that I may test them, whether they will walk in My law or not..... *17* Then the children of Israel did so and gathered, some more, some less. *19* And Moses said, "Let no one leave any of it till morning." *20* Notwithstanding they did not heed Moses. But some of them left part of it until morning, and it bred worms and stank. And Moses was angry with them. NKJV

Philippians 3: *13* Brethren, I do not count myself to have apprehended; but one thing I do, forgetting those things which are behind and reaching forward to those things which are ahead, *14* I press toward the goal for the prize of the upward call of God in Christ Jesus. NKJV

John 12: ⁴² Many people did believe in him, however, including some of the Jewish leaders. But they wouldn't admit it….. ⁴³ For they loved human praise more than the praise of God. NLT

Ephesians 6: ¹³ Therefore take up the whole armor of God, that you may be able to withstand in the evil day, and having done all, to stand. ¹⁴ Stand therefore,…NKJV

FOREWORD

As the Head Coach of a Division I football team, I understand all of the efforts needed to prepare a team for competition. The time recruiting the best professionals for your coaching staff, recruiting the right athletes who are gifted to play the sport, strength coaches to help prepare the athletes physically, athletic trainers to treat and prevent injuries, team meetings and practices to prepare the players mentally and all of the nutrition, equipment and logistics that are all involved in preparing a team for gameday. Just as important, however, is the spiritual development of the team. All of the aforementioned efforts will not be enough during a game; particularly when adversity comes to the players and coaches individually and/or collectively. This is why most teams encourage players to involve themselves in activities that will foster their spiritual growth, e.g., FCA, Bible study, team devotionals, prayer and attending church services. Moreover, it is my duty to provide a message that will encourage and prepare them for competition on gameday. This is not a simple matter as the message should fit the team and the challenge the team will face on each respective gameday. My constant prayer is that the Lord provide me with the right person (myself or someone else) and message to give the team. I was blessed to have Dr. Deland Myers serve as my Team Chaplain for three years and he delivered that message to our football team before every game. I watched and listened attentively as he used God's Word to provide our young men with not only the confidence to go out and perform at a high level, but also the assurance that they were already champions because they received Christ as their personal Lord and Savior. This book that Dr. Myers has written will be an excellent tool to me and likeminded coaches who strive to win and know the importance of gameday spiritual preparation. This will assist me in continuing to find a message that bests fit my team for the challenges that we will face and give me peace to know that I have done all I need to do to prepare my team. I look forward to using this book for gameday or any other situation where I need a message from God's Holy Word to prepare my team spiritually.

Willie Simmons
Head Football Coach
Florida A&M University

PREFACE

When I joined North Dakota State as the Director of the School of Food Systems, and my wife Evie as the Director of Equity and Diversity in the fall of 2007, I was called into the Office of then-President Joseph Chapman and asked to become the Faculty Athletic Representative for the Athletic Department replacing the previous faculty member who had left the university. Working with the Athletic Department was not something unknown to me since my wife Evie and I had worked with the Athletics Office at our previous place of employment, Iowa State University, in support of student-athletes, particularly student-athletes of color. I had not ever been asked to serve student-athletes in an official capacity; not to mention reporting directly to the President. In taking the role I gained unprecedented access to working with Athletics Administration, under the Direction of Gene Taylor, and Coaches. One Coach that I developed particularly strong ties with was Head Football Coach Craig Bohl. North Dakota State was in its infancy of becoming an NCAA Division I program after moving up from Division II and Coach Bohl had begun to build the foundation of one of the most storied Football Dynasties in NCAA Football History winning 9 NCAA National Football Championships from 2011 – 2021. Since his team had the largest number of students of color, we developed a unique relationship as I offered my support and ideas to assist his players.

Before one of his games, I was asked to do something I had never done before. Coach Bohl, like many college football coaches, held a Chapel Service for his players before the beginning of each game. On this Saturday, I was asked to lead a Chapel Service for the players. Leading a worship service was not unknown to me as I had been ordained as a minister in 2005 and started 2 churches, New Birth Baptist Church, one in Ames, Iowa where we previously resided, and Fargo, North Dakota where we were living. I had not, however, ever led a service for a football team before a game as I did not serve in the capacity of a Team Chaplain or provide spiritual support and guidance for an entire team. When I asked Coach Bohl what the nature of my message would be to the team, the response I received was to prepare the players for the game. At that point I began to think to myself, what could I offer a team of football players to prepare them to compete at the Division I Football level and what scripture(s) would I use to prepare them?

As a minister, I did understand that we as human beings exist in 3 parts; body, mind, and spirit.

Moreover, to have a victorious Christian life, all 3 of these parts had to be in alignment and control, otherwise, the enemy will cause you to become weak and you will succumb to the challenges/temptations you are presented with and will ultimately fall.

I began to understand what Coach Bohl and the other coaches understood, to develop players with the ability to compete in sports at the highest levels, all 3 of these parts also needed to be strengthened and developed. Coach Bohl and his football staff including assistant coaches, strength coaches, and trainers had been working diligently all week preparing the team physically and mentally with workouts, practices, film sessions, and game planning to prepare the team for their opponent. Moreover, on Saturday before the game, they would go over all that they had prepared for to ensure that everyone knew their roles, the importance of what they had been taught, and the game they were prepared to play. What he needed was something to prepare their spirit. Many of the players and coaches were believers and had been praying, reading their Bible, and attending weekly services and or bible studies at their local churches and/or Christian Student Organizations on campus such as The Fellowship of Christian Athletes. The coach was looking for the final word of preparation to prepare their spirits on Gameday.

With this understanding, I was honored that he would choose me to give this message to his players and I felt a tremendous responsibility with the knowledge that what I shared with the team could have a tremendous impact on how the players performed that day. With this in mind, I began to pray to ask the Lord to lead me to the right scriptures and message that I needed to prepare the team for the competition they would encounter. I was immediately led to the writings of the Apostle Paul who I believe from the scriptures show that he was a sports fan and very familiar with the training of athletes. Paul uses numerous metaphors in the Bible relating to sports including fighting, running a race, training, and being disqualified. The most familiar scripture that contains many of these metaphors is 1 Corinthians 9:24-27 (NKJV) "**24** Do you not know that those who run in a race all run, but one receives the prize? Run in such a way that you may obtain *it*. **25** And everyone who competes *for the prize* is temperate in all things. Now they *do it* to obtain a perishable crown, but we *for* an imperishable *crown*. **26** Therefore I run thus: not with uncertainty. Thus, I fight: not as *one who* beats the air. **27** But I discipline my body and bring *it* into subjection, lest, when I have preached to others, I myself should become disqualified." With this in mind, I understood that the adversity that one faces in life as a believer and the adversity that one faces in a sports contest are very similar and with that, I began to develop messages for the North Dakota State Football Team in their Chapel Services when given the opportunity for Coach Bohl and later Coach Kris Kleiman. The Lord continued to develop me over the years to provide Gameday messages for the team.

When I moved to Prairie View A&M University as the Endowed Professor of Food Systems in the College of Agriculture and Human Sciences in the Fall of 2015, I maintained an interest in supporting student-athletes, and upon my arrival, I found that two of the assistant football coaches, Reggie Moore, Wide Receivers Coach, and Willie Mack Garza, Defensive Backs Coach, were members of the new football staff that had recently been hired by then Head Coach Willie Simmons. I knew both Coach Moore and Garza from the time they were on the coaching staff with Coach Bohl at North Dakota State. Coach Simmons had just arrived on campus and he had put together his coaching staff and had not yet hired a Team Chaplain. I was introduced to Coach Simmons by Coach Moore and he invited me to give a message to the team as they began fall practice. By the grace of God, this meeting was "ordained" by God as we immediately developed a working and friendly relationship along with the relationship developed between his wife, Shaia and Evie. After that meeting, he invited me to serve as his Team Chaplain.

Due to his selection of myself as Team Chaplain, The Lord through the power of the Holy Spirit, continued to develop my ability to prepare messages for the teams on Gameday.

Being the Team Chaplain for the Football Team at Prairie View University was different than the relationship of a Football Team as a Faculty Athletic Representative. Coach Simmons requested that I be more closely involved in the spiritual development of the team not only on Gameday but throughout the week. To do this, he allowed me unfettered access to the team.

I was able to attend all practices, and team meetings, and traveled with the team. That included providing any needed support during study hall while traveling. Given this access, I developed a relationship with many of the players, met many of their family members, and provided spiritual support for them during times of sickness, injury, and bereavement for loved ones who passed away during and after the season. Moreover, by attending practices, team meetings, and all games, I learned more about their opponents and the challenges they would be facing. Because of this, I was able to develop Gameday messages more tailored to the needs of the team and the opponents they would be facing.

Messages that would provide support, encouragement, and yes, challenge the team. Coach Simmons and I worked in such close tandem with each other that he would use the Chapel Message as a "springboard" to give his final message to the team before the game. He shared with me how vital these Gameday messages were to the team to prepare them spiritually before they took the field for competition.

When Coach Simmons took the Head Coaching position at Florida A&M University, Coach Eric Dooley became Head Football Coach at Prairie View A&M University. Not knowing if I would keep the same position with Coach Dooley, I met with him and he agreed to allow me to stay on as Team Chaplain. Coach Dooley, like Coach Simmons, continued to allow me access to the team in all facets of the team preparation and Gameday. Coach Dooley took the spiritual development of the team and staff to another level.

Coach Dooley asked that I lead a weekly Bible Study for the Coaching Staff with the mindset that spiritual development for the coaches, along with the players, was also vital to the spiritual development of the team. If they, the coaches, were to be role models and leaders in the development of the body, mind, and spirit of the players, they needed to have their spirits ready also.

Coach Dooley also took the Chapel Service to another level. He referred to Chapel Service as a "Church Service". All seniors on the team led music before the Chapel Message, similar to what I encountered in a typical Sunday worship service. This required me to continue to develop my Chapel messages with the right scriptures that would continue to build on the "spiritual fire" developed by the music before the message. Coach Dooley also continued to stress the importance of the message before the game to prepare the spirits of the players before the competition.

May I also point out that through those messages, many of the players who were believers grew in their faith, while others became believers in the Lord Jesus Christ. In fact, some of them are ministers today and share the word of faith with others in many parts of the country in traditional and online church services.

I thank all of these coaches for their faith in me to provide Gameday messages for games at all levels including the Spring football Game, major rivalry games, divisional championship games, and NCAA Division I National Championship Games. These experiences over the past 16 years helped me to understand the challenges the coaches and their staff face to prepare teams for major college football competitions and the challenge the players have to prepare themselves to play as individuals and as a team. With this knowledge and experience, I have a very keen understanding of how important that 10 to 15-minute Team Chapel message is to the team in preparing them for competition.

This understanding led me to write this book for those who are being asked to prepare a message for a team on Gameday. This book does not explain how important the spiritual development of the individuals on a team, including coaches and training staff, is to the success of a team; those who use this book already know this. This book should be used as a tool to help prepare a message for a team primarily on Gameday; but can be used whenever a team or individual needs scripture to embolden their spirit. This book contains 40 messages based on scriptures that the Holy Spirit led me to develop that I believe can be used by someone preparing a Gameday Message; those persons could include Team Chaplains and ministers, coaches, or others who are being asked to give the Gameday message for all sports. The messages in this book can be used verbatim or as a guide to how the verse(s) could be used to prepare the spirit of a team prior to competition. Moreover, I believe the messages will feed the spirit of those who are believers and spark the interest of those who are not believers to learn more about the power that Christ has to strengthen them not only on Gameday and throughout life AND lead them to commit faith in our Lord and Savior Jesus Christ. My prayer is that you find this Gameday book helpful in the continued development of teams and help them to be fully prepared for competition on Gameday.

PROLOGUE

The purpose of this book is to be used by coaches, team chaplains, and anyone else who works with student-athletes as a supplement to prepare the Spirits of you and your team as you get ready for competition on the day of the game, e.g., Gameday. This book will not guarantee victory, freedom from mistakes, bad officiating calls, or increasing the player's or team's statistics during the game. I believe, however, that what this book will do is provide you with messages to prepare the spirit of the team, individually and collectively, for the day of competition to supplement all of the efforts that have been put in to prepare your team physically, mentally, and spiritually. The book will especially prepare those players and coaches who are believers and know that the spirit of God is in them. And because that spirit is in them, there is nothing that they cannot accomplish through the gifts that God has given them. Moreover, they can focus on the game knowing that God is taking care of all of their needs on and off the field through faith, and therefore they will be able to play with maximum focus and effort. The words shared in this book will encourage them to overcome the adversity that they will face. Yes, adversity is indeed something that all the players will face, whether from the opponents, the officials, the weather, crowds, and yes, even their teammates. The words shared in this book will help them through all these things to help prepare them for maximum effort and efficiency as they compete.

As a coach, you have put in numerous hours and effort to prepare your team for competition. As leaders, you should use the words of this book to reinforce the things that you have already shared with them. Moreover, the things that face the players will also impact them during the game including off-the-field concerns, the questioning of their ability, adversity from a variety of sources, and yes although you may not like to accept it, some anxiety. All of the aforementioned could impact your judgment, patience, and decision-making.

The purpose of the book is to assist you as well in these areas so that you can coach to the best of your ability so that your spirit is not compromised as you lead your team into the competition.

The book is broken into 40 different messages and all messages are not for every game; no different than your game plans are for every team that you compete against. As the leader of the team, you can choose the message that best suits the game that you are involved in and use your own words and situations to make the message relevant to your team.

REVEREND DR. DELAND J. MYERS SR. PH.D.

INTRODUCTION

Gameday is a unique time for all athletes. It is time when all of their efforts are focused on the purpose of competition and winning the game that is at hand. These include a) The time that has been put into the body by weight training and aerobic exercise to build endurance; b) the nutrients in the food consumed to get the body prepared to be at a peak performance level; c) the practices that focus on skill improvement and d) the position and team meetings to study your opponent that leads to the game plan. All of these aforementioned efforts come together to compete on the field of competition on what we call Gameday.

There is another aspect of Gameday, however, that must not be overlooked. In addition to the mental and physical aspects of the game, there is also the spiritual. As a believer in the Lord Jesus Christ, I and many coaches believe that we are not only mental and physical persons but also spiritual. The coaches that I have worked with believe that to compete at the highest levels you must consider the spiritual side as well.

In addition to all the things that are done to prepare that body physically and mentally to compete at the highest levels, you must also consider the spiritual side. To enhance this part of game preparation, I would like to suggest the following activities that can be considered to prepare the spiritual side of players and coaches:

1. Scripture Reading (The Spiritual Playbook) – The purpose of scripture reading is to know more about who we are as spiritual beings and how The Lord through the power of the Holy Spirit, can prepare an athlete for competition. Moreover, one can learn more about the promises that God has given us to

keep watch over players through their classes and to balance their lives between athletics and academics. If there are family responsibilities, including having children of their own, how all of these responsibilities can be managed while preparing for competition. God's Word gives tremendous promises to lean on when times become difficult and challenging and the Holy Spirit is a Helper who can help you through adversity. The Bible also provides assurances that even when we make mistakes, the Lord forgives through the blood of our Lord and Savior Jesus Christ and we can move on without the burden of guilt.

2. Prayer and Meditation – The Christian faith is not a religion! The Christian faith is a personal relationship with a living Savior who walks and talks with us. We communicate with our Lord and Savior through prayer. The Word tells us that we should always pray and never quit (Luke 18:1).

    God provides you with direction in all parts of your life and provides insight into what you have read in the Bible and gives you the day-to-day application of God's Word. Moreover, prayer is what will help an athlete through the trials of preparing for competition. Weight training and aerobic exercise can be a grueling process and puts tremendous strain on the body. The athlete can turn to prayer to get them through those difficult times. Prayer not only helps the athlete through physical preparation but also on the academic and personal side to help them through their classes and those personal situations that will inevitably happen while preparing themselves to compete.

3. Fellowship – Most student-athletes are prepared to compete as a team to meet their goals throughout their training and also on Gameday. The spiritual side of preparation is no different. Fellowship with other believers is critical (Hebrews 10:24-25). Some things happen in our lives where the encouragement of others is very helpful. Moreover, there will be those in the fellowship who can provide insight into what may be happening

that they aren't able to see. God provides the fellowship of other believers who can be with us and provide us with this additional insight. Athletes typically look to fellow teammates to lift them up when they are having a difficult practice, during weight training, and study table and/or a shoulder to lean on during a difficult time with personal issues; the fellowship of believers is no different. Being around fellow believers is important for the growth of the person spiritually.

During fellowship with other believers, you can gain insight into the scriptures that are being read, provides an opportunity to pray for and with others, and get valuable advice in making better choices in situations such as relationships, finances, etc. Moreover, a fellow believer may have been, or is currently, going through similar challenges that the athlete is going through and help them appropriately manage those issues.

This book is a supplement to all of these efforts and will provide the athlete, and their coaches, with words of encouragement, insight, and strength as they prepare for Gameday.

1

WHO ARE YOU?

Acts 19: [15] And the evil spirit answered and said, "Jesus I know, and Paul I know; but who are you?" NKJV

Acts 19 tells the story of seven men who attempted to drive demons out of a man as they had heard that Jesus had done and heard and/or seen Paul do. But when challenged by the demon if they had "what it takes" to drive him out as Jesus and Paul drove out demons they had no answer and were soundly defeated. In their response to the enemy they wanted to do something Jesus and Paul did but did not have a strong belief in Christ and His power (Acts 19:13) and it showed when challenged. This happens in our life as we seek to have victory in our lives when challenged by the enemy in the issues we face in life, e.g. family and personal relationships, finances, professional, and even health. If we don't have a strong belief in Christ and His power in our hearts when challenged, we will be soundly defeated and not have the victory in life that Christ has promised us.

As you prepare for your game today, you will be facing an opponent who will challenge your team with this very question: Who Are You? This will particularly be true if the opponent has had tremendous success and all indications and predictions by the experts are that you do not have a chance to win. The other teams they have played and will play they are more concerned about but, who are you? The question your opponent is asking is one about what you believe in your heart.

Do you believe you can defeat your opponent today? Do you believe in your physical preparation? Do believe in your mental preparation and game planning? Do you believe in your abilities and gifts as athletes? You must be confident as you are challenged today to compete against high-caliber competition. Let the other team know who you are! Remember, how you have been prepared mentally, physically, and spiritually. There should be no doubt or lack of confidence in who you are and what you believe. Finally, know that you can trust your coaches and teammates and have faith in their abilities. The bottom line, however, is that no one can answer that question but you as a player and as a team. Who are you?

NOTES

_____

_____

_____

_____

_____

_____

_____

_____

_____

_____

_____

_____

_____

_____

_____

_____

_____

_____

_____

_____

_____

_____

_____

Acts 19: ¹⁵ "And the evil spirit answered and said, "Jesus I know, and Paul I know; but who are you?" NKJV

2

GAMEDAY PREPARATION

1 Peter 5: ⁶ Therefore humble yourselves under the mighty hand of God, that He may exalt you in due time, ⁷ casting all your care upon Him, for He cares for you. ⁸ Be sober, be vigilant; because your adversary the devil walks about like a roaring lion, seeking whom he may devour. NKJV

1 Peter was written to encourage Christians who were undergoing persecution for their faith. In 1 Peter 5:6-8, he writes to provide them direction to approach every day to be victorious and keep their faith in the midst of persecution. In these verses, I also find encouragement and direction for teams as they prepare to compete. Let's examine each one:

Verse 6 – Humble yourselves and let God lift you up in due time. You must remember it is not about you but the goals of the team. Playing time, your roles, statistics, etc. are secondary to the goals of the team. You must forget about yourself and think of the team. Moreover, let God lift you up; not yourself. God will allow it to happen, not you.

Verse 7 – Place *all* your cares on Him for He cares for you. As you prepare for competition, other things in your life have not stopped including concerns about your family, finances, relationships, classes, etc. These things can take your focus off the game if you are not careful. Peter says place your cares on Jesus. He, has the power to handle any situation because nothing is too hard for him. Moreover, if he cares for us, He will use His power to handle any cares you have. Leave your cares with Him and get focused on the game.

Verse 8 – Be sober and be vigilant as your adversary is as a lion seeking to destroy you. First, Peter warns you to keep your mind clear (sober) and allow nothing to interrupt your focus on your game, e.g., the crowd, the media, your opponent, etc. Then you need to be vigilant – Don't let up for one second; if you do, the opportunity to get you off your game is there. Moreover, Peter says your enemy is like a lion looking for an opportunity to get you off of your game. The prey the lion hunts for is not focused on their surroundings and strays away from the pack and gets destroyed by the lion. If you are not focused on your task and goals during the game, your opponent, like a lion, will destroy you also. Therefore, team members must look out after each other to make sure teammates keep their focus.

These words of wisdom from Peter to help keep you grounded and focused on the task at hand today. Listen and embrace these words as you prepare on this Gameday.

NOTES

_____

_____

_____

_____

_____

_____

_____

_____

_____

_____

_____

_____

_____

_____

_____

_____

_____

_____

_____

_____

1 Peter 5: ⁶ Therefore humble yourselves under the mighty hand of God, that He may exalt you in due time, ⁷ casting all your care upon Him, for He cares for you. ⁸ Be sober, be vigilant; because your adversary the devil walks about like a roaring lion, seeking whom he may devour. NKJV

REVEREND DR. DELAND J. MYERS SR. PH.D.

3

PLAY WITH PURPOSE

1 Corinthians 9: ²⁴ Do you not know that those who run in a race all run, but one receives the prize? Run in such a way that you may obtain it. ²⁵ And everyone who competes for the prize is temperate in all things. Now they do it to obtain a perishable crown, but we for an imperishable crown. ²⁶ Therefore I run thus: not with uncertainty. Thus, I fight: not as one who beats the air. NKJV

Paul says as a believer we are all striving to see the blessings of God in our life and to overcome the challenges that we face. Moreover, he says that like in a race, everyone says they want to win but only those who strive and put in a total effort will truly be champions.

In today's game both you and your opponent have the same goals; to win the game. All of the players on each team, your team and your opponent, will say that they want to win as part of their overall team goals for the year. However, as Paul says, only those who are truly committed will achieve the goals that "they say" they want to reach. In 1 Corinthians 9:24-27, Paul gives the characteristics of those who are truly committed.

Paul says you first need to recognize that you have an opponent and they are striving to win; therefore, you need to be prepared for competition and play as if you know that other team also wants to win; so therefore you must play like you want to win!

Second, you need to be "temperate or disciplined" in everything you do. Therefore, you must be disciplined in all of your efforts to prepare for the game.

This includes your eating habits, how you go through pre-game workouts, staying focused in pre-game meetings, and working with trainers to get your body in condition. Moreover, Paul says that everything you do should do everything with purpose. Not just be disciplined, but know why you need to be disciplined. Not just follow what the coaches and trainers say to do but know why you are doing what you are doing to make sure that everything you do leads to your ultimate goal.

Finally, he says he does not run with uncertainty but with certainty and confidence so that when you are challenged on the field, know that you have indeed prepared for this game and can play with confidence.

As you prepare for this game, following the words of Paul, understand what it takes to be a winner in life and in this game today: being disciplined in everything you do, understanding the purpose in everything that you do, and having the confidence to trust in everything that you are doing. These are the true characteristics who are competing to win!

NOTES

_____

_____

_____

_____

_____

_____

_____

_____

_____

_____

_____

_____

_____

_____

_____

_____

_____

_____

_____

_____

_____

1 Corinthians 9: ²⁴ Do you not know that those who run in a race all run, but one receives the prize? Run in such a way that you may obtain it…. ²⁶ …Thus, I fight: not as one who beats the air. NKJV

4

WHAT DO YOU SAY?

Matthew 16: [13] When Jesus came into the region of Caesarea Philippi, He asked His disciples, saying, "Who do men say that I, the Son of Man, am?" [14] So they said, "Some say John the Baptist, some Elijah, and others Jeremiah or one of the prophets." [15] He said to them, "But who do you say that I am?" [16] Simon Peter answered and said, "You are the Christ, the Son of the living God." NKJV

Jesus had been spending time with His disciples teaching and training them about the Kingdom of God. During this time, he showed them miracles and the power of God to overcome all the issues of this life. At this point, Jesus asked them who the world said that He was and each had quick responses to what the world said. For Jesus to prepare them for what He wanted them to do, He needed to know who they thought He was. But when He asked them who He was, only one person, Simon Peter, had a response which happened to be the correct one; The Christ, Son of the Living God. When you think of the fact that Christ had been showing the disciples the power of God through his teaching and miracles, the fact that only one disciple stated who He is was very surprising. You would have thought they would have been able to see indeed that He was and is The Christ.

On this gameday, think of what your coaches have been doing with you individually and collectively as a team to prepare you for this season and the game today. If someone were to ask others about your team, I can guarantee you that there will be plenty of responses; from the media, coaches in your conference, and even your fans who follow and support you will have a response. They would break down your strengths, your weaknesses, and your prospects for success. But, if I asked you, individually and collectively as a team, who are you as a team what would you say? Like Jesus with His team, the disciples, what others say does not matter.

What really should and will affect your performance is what you say about yourself.

In light of all that the coaches have taught you, in light of all the preparation you have been through, and the talents and gifts that are present on this team, what would you say? Do you have a response? Do you know who you are as a team and what your capabilities are? I am sure your opponents have reviewed the film and made a decision about who you are, and more importantly how to defeat you. Will you respond like Peter, e.g., yes, I know who we are; yes, I know what our capabilities are individually and collectively, and yes we are capable of defeating any opponent that we face.

As you prepare, do not anyone else define you. You must be able to define yourself and have confidence to go out and execute what you have been prepared to do. When you take the field today there will be plenty of opinions out there about you as a team, however, those opinions really don't matter. The question being asked about you as a team is, *what do you say?*

NOTES

_____

_____

_____

_____

_____

_____

_____

_____

_____

_____

_____

_____

_____

_____

_____

_____

_____

Matthew 16: [13] ....He asked His disciples, saying, "Who do men say that I, the Son of Man, am?" [14] So they said, "Some say John the Baptist, some Elijah, and others Jeremiah or one of the prophets." [15] He said to them, "But who do you say that I am?" [16] Simon Peter answered and said, "You are the Christ, the Son of the living God." NKJV

5

MANAGE IT

*Genesis 4: ⁶ So the L*ORD *said to Cain, "Why are you angry? And why has your countenance fallen? ⁷ If you do well, will you not be accepted? And if you do not do well, sin lies at the door. And its desire is for you, but you should rule over it." NKJV*

God had outlined to Cain and His brother Abel what they were supposed to do to fulfill God's requirement for him to receive His blessing. Abel brought the best of what he had and God was pleased. Cain brought not his best, but just some of what he had, and God was displeased. Unfortunately, Cain became upset with God because He was displeased. God then told Cain he knew what was required so he shouldn't be upset. He needed to do what was required and manage his emotions before they got him in trouble. Unfortunately, Cain did not listen and satan used his lack of control to hurt his brother Abel.

Like Cain, we all have weaknesses that we need to address. In today's game, examine yourself as a player on this team. You have strengths and you also have weaknesses; some of them have been pointed out to you by coaches and fellow teammates. Sometimes we don't want to address those things because we believe they are a sign of weakness. If we don't address them, however, your opponent can use the weakness against you in the game today and it could be disastrous to yourself and the team. These weaknesses could be a certain technique that you need to master, losing control of your leading to a lack of attention to detail and/ or resulting in penalties during the game and/or over or underconfident in your abilities or those of your coaches and teammates.

As you prepare for today's game, I challenge you to think of those areas that you have been asked to be aware of that are weaknesses in your game that your opponent can and could hurt the team's chances for success.

Consider addressing them by doing the following: 1) what is that area or areas that you need to be aware of that are ones you need to work on and improve in your game; 2) let the coach know that you have been working on that aspect of your game and are ready to receive any coaching support or advice to help you manage this part of your game; 3) be ready receive advice and without anger or frustration knowing it is not personal but beneficial to your growth and success as a player and team; 4) pray that the Lord give you strength to overcome any shortcomings that you have.

In today's game, don't let your opponent exploit areas that you need to work on. As the Lord implored Cain to do, I implore you not to forget or ignore them and think they will just "go away". Recognize, address, and pray about them in order to be successful. *Manage it!*

NOTES

_____

_____

_____

_____

_____

_____

_____

_____

_____

_____

_____

_____

_____

_____

_____

_____

_____

_____

_____

_____

_____

*Genesis 4: ⁶ So the L*ORD *said to Cain, "Why are you angry? And why has your countenance fallen? ⁷ If you do well, will you not be accepted? And if you do not do well, sin lies at the door. And its desire is for you, but you should rule over it." NKJV*

6

TODAY'S GAME IS A NEW GAME

Exodus 16: [4] Then the LORD said to Moses, "Behold, I will rain bread from heaven for you. And the people shall go out and gather a certain quota every day, that I may test them, whether they will walk in My law or not….. [17] Then the children of Israel did so and gathered, some more, some less. [19] And Moses said, "Let no one leave any of it till morning." [20] Notwithstanding they did not heed Moses. But some of them left part of it until morning, and it bred worms and stank. And Moses was angry with them. NKJV

When God freed the children of Israel, He put them in the wilderness to test them to see if they were worthy to enter into the Promised Land God. He also provided everything they needed.

One thing he provided was bread, or manna, every day for them. It provided everything they needed for the day, however, if they tried to use it the next day, except for the sixth day because they could not work on the seventh or Sabbath day, it would turn rotten. Unfortunately, some of the people did not listen to God, through Moses, and the manna rotted which made Moses very angry.

As you approach the game today, you individually and as a team, may have been very successful in your previous game(s). The game plan, the team effort, and the individual accomplishments were indeed outstanding. However, let me warn you that this was "yesterday's manna". Those things that made you successful before had for them. you can't live on for today's game. You will need some "fresh manna".

Your opponent will not have any recognition or respect for what you did last week or even yesterday. The same maximum effort that you used in the previous game(s) to be successful will have to be at the very least duplicated and probably exceeded to be successful today. The hard work, discipline, attention to detail selflessness, and confidence you will need today. Make sure you respect your opponent and don't think that the "manna" or effort today will be easier than it has been previously. If you, like the children of Israel, do not heed these words, the danger is that you will go out and "stink up" the field with your less-than-maximum effort which will lead to disastrous results which I am sure will make your leaders, e.g., coaches like Moses, very unhappy. So today, on this Gameday, my advice to you is not to rely on your past efforts or any reputation from your last game(s). Put in the work, stay focused, be committed to team unity; and *get some fresh manna.*

NOTES

_____

_____

_____

_____

_____

_____

_____

_____

_____

_____

_____

_____

_____

_____

_____

*Exodus 16: ⁴ Then the L*ORD *said to Moses, "Behold, I will rain bread from heaven for you. And the people shall go out and gather a certain quota every day, that I may test them, whether they will walk in My law or not….. ¹⁷ Then the children of Israel did so and gathered, some more, some less. ¹⁹ And Moses said, "Let no one leave any of it till morning." ²⁰ Notwithstanding they did not heed Moses. But some of them left part of it until morning, and it bred worms and stank. And Moses was angry with them. NKJV*

REVEREND DR. DELAND J. MYERS SR. PH.D.

7

PRESS ON

Philippians 3:13 Brethren, I do not count myself to have apprehended; but one thing I do, forgetting those things which are behind and reaching forward to those things which are ahead, 14 I press toward the goal for the prize of the upward call of God in Christ Jesus. NKJV

Paul was encouraging the people of the church at Philippi to live out their faith in the Lord Jesus Christ. Paul told them that he had goals that he wanted to accomplish as a Christian and through his best efforts he had not yet obtained or reached where he wanted to be (Philippians 3:10-12). He said that although he had not reached where he wanted to be, to get to where he wanted to be he had to forget those things that had happened and "press on" or move forward toward those goals that he was striving for through Jesus Christ.

As you prepare for today's game, have you assessed where you are as a team individually and collectively? I am sure that you have goals that you want to accomplish for the upcoming season. Some of these probably include improvements in your overall play on the field, improved conditioning, placing yourself at the top of your league, etc. If are truly honest with yourselves, you will admit that have not achieved all of these goals. The question now is, how will you proceed with the rest of the season, including this game?

Paul gives us the formula/blueprint on how to proceed with the same energy you started with keeping these goals in mind. The first thing he says is, to be honest with yourself and realize that you are not where you want to be. The second step is then to put the past behind you, particularly your disappointments that can prevent you from moving forward. One famous coach said, "Never let the same team beat you twice" meaning if you dwell on past shortcomings, you will never be able to move forward. You must keep going with the same commitment and focus or the past could also leave you behind or even be regressing. Finally, Paul says "Press on". Note, that he did not say "run on" or even "walk on". The word press means that as you proceed toward the goals that you have set, there will be obstacles and challenges that you will have to push your way through. It has not been easy this far and will not be, however, if you accept this and decide that these will not stop you from moving forward you can reach your goals.

So, as you prepare for today's game keep in mind who you are as a team collectively. What were your goals when you started? Where are you now? Press on towards those goals and do not let the challenges of the game today keep you from achieving your goals, be it the opponent, the officials, injuries, weather or past mistakes etc.. Keep your *eyes on the prize* team, no matter the obstacles and *press on*!

NOTES

_____
_____
_____
_____
_____
_____
_____
_____
_____
_____
_____
_____
_____
_____
_____
_____
_____
_____
_____

Philippians 3: [13] Brethren, I do not count myself to have apprehended; but one thing I do, forgetting those things which are behind and reaching forward to those things which are ahead, [14] I press toward the goal for the prize of the upward call of God in Christ Jesus. NKJV

8

DON'T BE OUT OF POSITION

2 Samuel 11: [1] It happened in the spring of the year, at the time when kings go out to battle, that David sent Joab and his servants with him, and all Israel; and they destroyed the people of Ammon and besieged Rabbah. But David remained at Jerusalem. NKJV

David was the greatest King in the history of Israel. He had the looks, intelligence, and fearlessness, and accomplished probably the greatest victory by one person in the history of the country by defeating the giant Goliath. Moreover, he was handpicked by God to be the King of Israel and called by God a "man after God's own heart (1 Samuel 13:14)". Therefore, he could not be defeated, right? No, that was wrong. He fell into an adulteress relationship with a woman, Bathsheba, which led to murder and the instability of the country.

This great man was brought down by not being where he was supposed to be, e.g., being "out of position". When he should have been with his soldiers he was at home. By being out of position, the enemy "set him up" to do things he should not have done. The Bible doesn't say why David was "out of position". Perhaps he lost his focus while he was at war. Maybe he did not respect his opponent and didn't think he would be needed. Or maybe he thought he was smarter than God and knew what was best. At any rate, he was out of position and the result was disastrous.

As you prepare for your opponent today, you have done everything you need to do to be successful. You have the right players, the right conditioning, and excellent practices with the best coaching and game planning. Like David however, all of your efforts individually and collectively can go for naught if your opponent gets you "out of position". Each player has been directed and warned about the scheming of the opponent. The game "tendencies" of the opponent, their key players, their strengths, and weaknesses. Every offensive and defensive play is designed for everyone to be in a certain place on each of those plays in response to what the opponent is doing. All of this planning will not work, however, if someone is out of position. Realize that your opponent today understands that you know about them and will plan to run "misdirection" plays with the expressed goal of getting you out of position.

In today's game, everyone must be on their guard to ensure that they are not out of position or it could cost the team the opportunity to win. This can happen by 1) not listening and losing your focus on what you were taught and practiced; 2) thinking that you can "make a play" based on your ability and not doing what you have been instructed to do; and/or 3) following your opponents "misdirection" plays as opposed to looking at your "keys" to help you understand what you are supposed to do. Today make sure you understand the importance of your game plan and be committed to what you have planned. Keep focused, remember your role as part of the team, and don't let your opponent catch you *"out of position"*.

NOTES

_____

_____

_____

_____

_____

_____

_____

_____

_____

_____

_____

_____

_____

_____

_____

_____

_____

_____

_____

2 Samuel 11: [1] It happened in the spring of the year, at the time when kings go out to battle, that David sent Joab and his servants with him, and all Israel; and they destroyed the people of Ammon and besieged Rabbah. But David remained at Jerusalem. NKJV

REVEREND DR. DELAND J. MYERS SR. PH.D.

9

HOW BAD DO YOU WANT IT?

Matthew 11: [12] And from the days of John the Baptist until now the kingdom of heaven suffers violence, and the violent take it by force. NKJV

In Matthew 11, Jesus eulogizes the great John the Baptist who was the forerunner of Jesus and prepared the way for Him to teach about the Kingdom of God and bring salvation to the world. During his eulogy, Jesus makes a very profound statement; he says those who want the kingdom must be committed, aggressive, eager, and willing to do "whatever it takes" to get the blessings of the kingdom at the expense of family, friends, and their own needs and desires (the violent take it by force). In other words, many say they want the blessings of the kingdom but only the committed actually receive them.

As you prepare for today's game, think about your goals and what you and your team are focusing on; both individually and collectively as a team. You must be aware, however, that other teams have the same goals also. The game that you are playing has become increasingly competitive. In addition to effort, there are new and improved methods in training, nutrition, practice facilities, stadium development, etc. In other words, all the teams that you will be playing against, including the team today, like you, all want to win. However, only those who are truly committed will actually achieve that goal. These persons are those who are willing to put in the practice time and get out of their comfort zone to learn new techniques, schemes, playbooks, and game plans. Moreover, those who are willing to sacrifice their time, old eating habits, and personal goals for the sake of the team, will grasp that championship and find themselves winners.

So today, are you truly committed to winning this game that you are about to play? Are you willing to put aside everything to focus on this game, e.g., relationships, fears, egos, etc.? Have you committed to the team goals at the expense of your own? Have you committed to the game plan and will you stay locked in on the game plan and not be tricked into stepping away from the plan regardless of what the opponent does? Have you committed yourself to keep your focus no matter the "trash talking" by the opponent and fans, calls by the officials, or being asked to sacrifice some of your playing time and accept possible game changes by the coaches? If you haven't you could be making a grave error and underestimating your opponent as you must assume that they will be making that commitment. Only the team that is truly committed to overcoming everything and staying true to their goals will win. Your challenge today individually and collectively is very basic but of ultimate importance: *"How Bad Do You Want It"*?

REVEREND DR. DELAND J. MYERS SR. PH.D.

NOTES

_____
_____
_____
_____
_____
_____
_____
_____
_____
_____
_____
_____
_____
_____
_____
_____
_____
_____
_____
_____
_____
_____
_____

Matthew 11: ¹² And from the days of John the Baptist until now the kingdom of heaven suffers violence, and the violent take it by force. NKJV

10

THE FOUR BE-ATTITUDES OF SUCCESS

1 Corinthians 16: [13] *Be on guard. Stand firm in the faith. Be courageous. Be strong. NLT*

In the Book of 1st Corinthians, Paul is seeking to direct the church he founded to get back to the focus of advancing faith and hope in Jesus Christ. In 1 Corinthians 16, Paul is completing his letter and gives the church 4 key areas of focus on to build a strong church; what I call 'Be-Attitudes". They informed them to be on their guard or be aware, stand on the faith in Jesus Christ, be courageous, and be strong. I have found these verses to be great foundational verses for many organizations. I call them the Be-Attitudes of success; not to be confused with the Beatitudes or blessings given by Jesus in the "Sermon on the Mount" (Matthew 5:1-12).

As you prepare for today's game, I believe these are the attitudes that will help you collectively and as individuals compete at the highest levels. The first is to *"Be Alert or Be Aware"*.

Make sure you have a keen awareness of who you are playing today, their strengths, and weaknesses. Know where you are playing and the impact of the crowd, weather, and the officials calling the game. Moreover, be aware of the importance of the game and how it will impact your overall team goals.

The second is to *"Be Faithful"*. No matter what you encounter today, stay true to who you are as an individual and collectively as a team. Do not let the opponent or situations change your character and what you stand for. Stay faithful to the game plan and what you have practiced during the week, albeit with some adjustments that will invariably be made during the game.

The third is *"Be Courageous"*. You must play fearlessly and when called upon to make a play, go and execute without trepidation or concern knowing you can do what you have been asked to do. Regarding this Be-Attitude, some translations say "Act like men or be mature". This means that you must take responsibility for your actions and not blame anyone else, moreover as a mature person you can take criticism without taking it personally, and keep your focus as well as helping other teammates keep their focus.

Finally, the fourth is to *"Be Strong"*. No matter how well you plan and how well prepared you are mentally, physically, and yes spiritually, there will be adversity and things that you have not planned for that you will have to work through. An unfortunate injury, a poor call by an official, poor weather or field conditions, etc. Decide before the game starts that whatever comes up, you individually and collectively will be strong enough to work your way through it and accomplish your goals.

These are words, from the Bible that can help you prepare you for today's game. I encourage you to embrace these Be-Attitudes and get prepared to win this game today.

NOTES

1 Corinthians 16: [13] Be on guard. Stand firm in the faith. Be courageous. Be strong. NLT

REVEREND DR. DELAND J. MYERS SR. PH.D.

11

WHAT ARE YOU LOOKING AT?

1 Samuel 16: [7] *"...For the* LORD *does not see as man sees; for man looks at the outward appearance, but the* LORD *looks at the heart." NKJV*

The account of David being anointed as King is covered in 1 Samuel 16. The Bible says that God sent the Prophet Samuel to find another king that He had chosen to replace the current king Saul. The scriptures that when Samuel arrived, David's father Jesse did not think David was the right choice because he was too small and too young. God, however, told Samuel do not look at David's outward appearance, God was more interested in his heart.

As you prepare for the game today individually and collectively, I would encourage you to have the "eyes of God" when you engage your opponent. Some of the biggest mistakes during competition are for a team not to respect the opponent by looking at their stature, the size of the organization, or the media reports that claim that one team is so superior to the other that it should be an "easy win". The results however are not always as "predicted".

This is because they did not take into account "the heart" of the opponent and their 'will to win". Be so very careful that you do not get caught in this trap of underestimating your opponent. Assume that they have the heart to do "whatever it takes" to compete against you and you need to be at your best at all times. Do not listen to the "Jesse's" of the world who claim to know who is better; you take into account the heart of your opponent and be ready to play.

The converse is also true. Your opponent could look at you and claim that you are no match for them collectively or at certain positions. They have better players, resources, experience, etc. that you are no match for them. My question to you is "What are you looking at?". Do you accept the words of "Jesse" that you are not good enough or do you accept the "words of God" who says "Look at your heart"? What is in your heart today? The Bible says as a person thinks in their heart, that is who they are (Proverbs 23:7).

What do you believe? Do you believe you can compete with your opponent individually and collectively? Do you believe that your preparation has prepared you to compete? My challenge to you today is that before you compete today and go through your checks of equipment, trainer's preparation of your body, pre-game meal, walk-through, etc., look at your heart. What do you believe? Make sure you do not underestimate your opponent and most importantly you do not underestimate yourself. *What are you looking at today?*

NOTES

_____

_____

_____

_____

_____

_____

_____

_____

_____

_____

_____

_____

_____

_____

_____

_____

_____

_____

_____

_____

_____

_____

1 Samuel 16: ⁷ "…For the LORD does not see as man sees; for man looks at the outward appearance, but the LORD looks at the heart." NKJV

12

LISTEN TO WISE COUNSEL

1 Kings 12: ⁸ "But he rejected the advice which the elders had given him, and consulted the young men who had grown up with him, who stood before him." NKJV

When Solomon died his son Rehoboam took his place. When preparing to lead the country the people were concerned about the direction of the nation and asked that he treat them in a more fair manner than his father Solomon. When faced with this decision under pressure, he asked the elders who served under his father who had more experience than he did. They said to listen to the voice of the people. He also asked the young men he grew up with their opinion and they said to make life harder for the people. He rejected the advice of the elders and took the advice of the younger men as a show of strength and it had disastrous results. Unfortunately, his Grandfather David made a similar critical error in not listening to the wise council (2 Samuel 11:3) as a show of control resulting in a relationship with a woman that caused disastrous results in the country.

In today's contest, you will be challenged with tough decisions during the game in a potentially hostile environment that will require you to make some very tough decisions. Some of these decisions will be ones that will need to be made in split seconds and the wrong decision could be disastrous to your team's goals today.

You will receive all manner of advice. Some from your teammates, coaches, and even from your mind. Moreover, you will have your opponent and or the crowd attempt to provoke you to retaliate or make a rash decision that will hurt your team. My advice to you today is that you commit yourself to listen to the "wise council" that you have as part of your team. Listen and do what your coaches have or will tell you during the game to make sure that you are making the correct call. You can also listen to teammates who have been identified by coaches and/or had more experience and been trustworthy throughout your time with the team. The absolute last thing you want to do is to make a rash decision out of anger, ego, or your thoughts that would go against what the "wise council" has told you to do.

So today as you enter a game that will be very competitive and will be in a potentially hostile environment from the stands and on the field, make sure you listen and commit in your heart and in your actions that you will listen and heed the words of wise council and not let emotions make your decisions for you that could lead to disastrous results for you and your team.

NOTES

_____

_____

_____

_____

_____

_____

_____

_____

_____

_____

_____

_____

_____

_____

_____

_____

_____

_____

_____

_____

_____

_____

_____

_____

1 Kings 12: ⁸ "But he rejected the advice which the elders had given him, and consulted the young men who had grown up with him, who stood before him." NKJV

13

KNOW YOUR ROLE

John 1: ⁶ "There was a man sent from God, whose name was John:... ⁸ He was not that Light, but was sent to bear witness of that Light." NKJV

One of the most important persons in all of The Bible was John the Baptist. John had a miraculous birth and the scripture said he was born with the Holy Spirit (Luke 1:15) which was rare considering that when we now accept Christ, we all have the Holy Spirit. Despite all of the great things that characterize John the Baptist, the Apostle John points out that he had a specific role, to bear witness of Jesus who is the Light of the World. The scriptures also tell us that when asked, John the Baptist made it clear he knew what his role was and embraced it (John 1:21-27). John was very successful in his mission. Jesus proceeded with His ministry in the way God intended including going to the cross to save us from our sins through the efforts of John the Baptist. Moreover, Jesus says that he was one of the greatest men who ever lived (Matthew 11:11)!

On every team, everyone has a role to play. As you prepare for your game today, the question is "Do you know your role?"; moreover "Do you embrace it"? As a member of this team, you are blessed with a gift to play this game at a very high level. Most people cannot play the game with the skill and ability that God has blessed you with. Many people are frankly in awe and wish they had the ability to compete at this level. However, given the nature of a team sport, everyone does not have the same role. Some will be on the field more than others. Some will be involved in more plays that get public recognition and visibility than others. Some roles are fluid and subject to change based on the game plan, the availability of other players, and game situations.

Despite what your role is, all coaches and team leaders agree that every person on the team is important and has a role and every person on the team must embrace this role to be successful today. The key to successful teams is that everyone accepts and embraces their role and like John the Baptist, executes it excellently and to the best of their ability. Some will be asked to execute and be required to be on the field for most of the game. Others will be called on for certain plays; such as special teams in football. Others will be called on to encourage and support those who are on the field for most of the game and to be ready if and when the situation in the game changes.

Your challenge today will be to know your role and embrace it with all that you have. All players should respect and support all players on the team, regardless of their role, and encourage each other. Moreover, realize that roles are fluid and are subject to change given what is needed for the team to be successful. Today, commit yourself to knowing and embrace your role and respect the role of all members of the team. *Do you know your role?*

NOTES

_____

_____

_____

_____

_____

_____

_____

_____

_____

_____

_____

_____

_____

_____

_____

_____

_____

_____

_____

_____

_____

_____

John 1: ⁶ "There was a man sent from God, whose name was John:… ⁸ He was not that Light, but was sent to bear witness of that Light." NKJV

14

YOU WERE BUILT FOR THIS

1 Samuel 17: [36] *Your servant has killed both lion and bear;
and this uncircumcised Philistine will be like one of them,
seeing he has defied the armies of the living God."* [37] *Moreover
David said, "The* LORD, *who delivered me from the paw of
the lion and from the paw of the bear, He will deliver me
from the hand of this Philistine." NKJV*

As a young man David was presented with a tremendous challenge;
to defeat the champion, Goliath. Everyone who witnessed this battle
including both the Israeli and Philistine soldiers and the King of
Israel himself, that David was outmatched. David, however, saw the
battle differently. He believed that he was able to defeat Goliath. His
assessment of his chances to win was not baseless. He informed King
Saul that as a young man, he had encountered both a lion and a bear
where he supposedly outmatched and won! Furthermore, David said
because he had been successful in these previous battles, the same God
that was with him then would be with him against Goliath and he
could defeat him. In other words, David said that "he had been built or
prepared for this day!"

On this gameday, I would encourage you to embrace that you have
been prepared for the competition you will face today. First of all, think
of all that you have been through to get you ready for this game today;
you have been built for this. Think of what you have had to do to get to
this point. Think of the intense conditioning, the careful consumption
of the right foods, the grueling practices, and the long game-planning
meetings you have been built for this!! Think of the competition that you
have faced to get on this team, those who challenged you and said that

you cannot compete at this level, some of you from difficult backgrounds where you grew up and difficult family and school situations that should have knocked you out and yet you are here; you have been built for this!! Think of the teams that you have faced so far in this season and/or previous seasons, difficult competition against opponents they said you could not compete against and you did so and gained the respect of those opponents; you have been built for this! Today, there are reports from the "so-called" experts that say you can't compete against this team. Like David, you should tell anyone, your detractors, your teammates, and even yourself, I have been built for this. There is no one person or team that I cannot compete against and win.

Today, embrace what you have done and where you have been taught and prepared for.

Embrace how God has gifted you to be at this point in your athletic career and he did not bring you to this point to not have you ready to compete against anyone. You have been through too much and have accomplished too much. Go and compete to win as if nothing is beyond your capabilities. You have proved it before and you will prove it again today! *You have been built for this!*

NOTES

_____
_____
_____
_____
_____
_____
_____
_____
_____
_____
_____
_____
_____
_____
_____
_____
_____
_____

1 Samuel 17: [36] Your servant has killed both lion and bear; and this uncircumcised Philistine will be like one of them, seeing he has defied the armies of the living God." [37] Moreover David said, "The LORD, who delivered me from the paw of the lion and from the paw of the bear, He will deliver me from the hand of this Philistine." NKJV

REVEREND DR. DELAND J. MYERS SR. PH.D.

15

HOW STRONG ARE YOU?

Proverbs 24: ¹⁰ If you faint in the day of adversity, Your strength is small. NKJV

In athletics, a tremendous amount of time, effort, and resources are invested in athletes to improve their strength. This is done to compete at the highest level with the competition.

State-of-the-art weight rooms, running tracks, and nutrition centers have been built as part of this effort. Experts in weight training, nutrition, and sports medicine have been hired in the hopes to develop and maintain the strength of the athletes. The results of all of these efforts are measured by a variety of different tests. These include the amount of weight that can be lifted, the speed at which the athletes can run along with their stamina, and recovery time are different ways to measure the strength of an athlete.

The Bible has many verses that discuss the importance of strength in our life as Christians and one very often quoted verse is Isaiah 40:31 which says "They that wait upon the Lord shall renew their strength" – KJV. The scripture found in Proverbs 24:10 however, gives us some insight on how God measures strength. Not by physical strength and stamina but by how you respond to adversity, trouble, or when things don't go "your way". The verse says if you quit, or shrink back, you are not very strong.

As you prepare for the game today, ask yourself, "How strong are you?". In any competition, there will be times when things may not go "your way". These could include a call by an official, getting behind on the scoreboard, weather conditions that make playing difficult, an unfortunate encounter with an opponent, or a change in the game plan that may reduce your playing time. The question is not whether these things could happen, the question is how you will respond. Will you keep your composure and focus on the game or lose your focus and/or become angry and lose your composure because of the adversity you are facing. Will you "keep the faith" in your ability and those of your teammates and coaches or begin to blame others for the challenges you are encountering? Will you continue to give 100% effort to overcome adversity or give less than a total effort because you don't think you can overcome the challenge? The Bible is clear on this subject and one that you need to keep in mind when you compete in the game today. Will you work to overcome any adversity you encounter today or will you "give up"? Will you show strength in the midst of the challenges today or weakness? The question for you today individually and collectively as a team is, *"How strong are you"*?

NOTES

_____

_____

_____

_____

_____

_____

_____

_____

_____

_____

_____

_____

_____

_____

_____

_____

_____

_____

_____

_____

_____

_____

Proverbs 24: ¹⁰ If you faint in the day of adversity, Your strength is small. NKJV

16

MAKE THE MOST OF YOUR OPPORTUNITY/ REDEEM THE TIME

Ephesians 5: ¹⁵ So be careful how you live. Don't live like fools, but like those who are wise. ¹⁶ Make the most of every opportunity... NLT

The Bible speaks of having the right perspective on life regarding opportunity and time. As a believer we must understand the importance of taking advantage of the opportunities that The Lord provides us with the realization that we need to grateful when these opportunities arise; not as an entitlement or expectation. You must understand that these opportunities do not last forever. There is a certain period of time you have to take advantage of the opportunity given to you. Jesus himself said that he must do the works that God The Father sent him to do "while it was day (with the time God gave him to complete it) for when the night comes (when the time was over) not even He would not be able to work anymore (John 9:4). This is the message Paul is giving us in Ephesians 5:15-16, e.g., don't be foolish and waste your opportunities/time. Take advantage of your opportunities ("redeem the time" in NKJV translation).

In athletics every gameday is an opportunity. You get the opportunity to show how well you can compete with the skills you have individually and collectively as a team. Today's game is an opportunity to work toward the team and personal goals that were set forth months and perhaps years ago. Moreover, this is an opportunity to play against a competitor who has the same desires that you have and be victorious. Understand that you don't have "all the time in the world"; the only time you have to take advantage of this opportunity is today!

Do not waste this opportunity that is available for you and your team today. Don't waste it worrying about the fans, conditions, and officiating. Don't waste it worrying about what the media and the experts have said, both positive and negative, and what happened in a previous game(s). Don't waste it worrying about your playing time, off the field issues, and how the game preparation might have not gone exactly perfect. Your major concern today is to take advantage of the opportunity to compete against your opponent in the time that God has provided for you! Get focused. Don't be foolish and miss this opportunity. Redeem the time you have and *take advantage of this opportunity today!*

NOTES

_____

_____

_____

_____

_____

_____

_____

_____

_____

_____

_____

_____

_____

_____

_____

_____

_____

_____

_____

Ephesians 5: ¹⁵ So be careful how you live. Don't live like fools, but like those who are wise. ¹⁶ Make the most of every opportunity… NLT

REVEREND DR. DELAND J. MYERS SR. PH.D.

17

PLAY YOUR GAME

1 Samuel 17: [38] Then Saul gave David his own armor—a bronze helmet and a coat of mail. [39] David put it on, strapped the sword over it, and took a step or two to see what it was like, for he had never worn such things before. "I can't go in these," he protested to Saul. "I'm not used to them." So David took them off again. NLT

The battle of David vs Goliath is one of the greatest accounts of battle strategy, courage and the power of God in a person's life ever recorded. One part of the story covers David's preparation to fight Goliath. There was a certain way that soldiers fought in those days, typically with armor, shield and some type of an offensive weapon such as a sword and/ or spear. King Saul, who agreed to let David be the soldier to challenge the champion Goliath, gave him his personal armor which would have been the best armor in the country. The scripture said however, that when David put on the armor it did not fit him and he refused to fight in it because he said this was not "use to them" and sought his own weapon; which was the slingshot. Basically, he was saying this is not the way I fight and I will not fight using your methods; I must fight my way, e.g., I must play my game!

In today's contest you may find that there are "so-called" experts, e,g., commentators, the media, fans, etc., who will tell you how to defeat today's opponent. Those "experts", however do not know you, your teammates and your coaches; nor do they understand your team culture and strategy that has been successful for you. Moreover, they do not know the gifts that God has blessed you with to compete; although these so called experts will claim they do. Do not fall into the trap of trying to play in a way that you have not prepared for and what your coaches have strategized for this game. Do not let your opponent, the fans, or even the officials take you out of your game; even though they may claim that they are trying to help you. These persons do not know what is best for you or your team. Stay with who you are as an individual and as a team and commit yourself to the game plan. Although there may be adjustments in the game plan during the game, the foundation of who you are and how you play will not change. Like David, know that you can win and that your game preparations have you ready to compete. Stay focused on your goals, compete to win and *play your game!*

NOTES

_____

_____

_____

_____

_____

_____

_____

_____

_____

_____

_____

_____

_____

_____

_____

_____

_____

_____

_____

1 Samuel 17: [38] Then Saul gave David his own armor—a bronze helmet and a coat of mail. [39] David put it on, strapped the sword over it, and took a step or two to see what it was like, for he had never worn such things before. "I can't go in these," he protested to Saul. "I'm not used to them." So David took them off again. NLT

18

STEP UP

Esther 4: [14] *For if you remain completely silent at this time, relief and deliverance will arise for the Jews from another place, but you and your father's house will perish. Yet who knows whether you have come to the kingdom for such a time as this?" NKJV*

The story of Esther is one of courage and faith of a woman who was called upon to save her people, the Jews. The King chose Esther to be the queen by the King of the country when the Jewish people were not in a position of power. There was one person in the kingdom who did not like the Jews and made plans to eliminate them from the country. Esther's Uncle Mordecai found out about this plot and said that because of the position Esther held, she had access to the king to stop this from happening. When Esther said this was not her role and she was not sure if she could do this, her uncle's response in Esther 4:14 was that perhaps God had put her in this position for a time such as this; in other words, Esther you need to "step up".

In today's game, as in other games, situations arise that require someone or a group of persons on the team to do something perhaps they did not know they would be called upon to do or even know if it is within their capability to do. Perhaps a player gets hurt or is removed from the game and someone has to take their place. Maybe there is an in-game strategy change that requires one or more persons on the team to play more or in a different role than they had intended. Or perhaps there is a key part of the game that a play has to be made to maintain or change the momentum of the game in your favor. In these situations, a player or group of players on the team must be ready to perform or "step up". Even if this is not what you normally do, or don't have the experience that some others have on the team, today you may be called to "step up".

Therefore, in today's game, commit yourself to be ready if called upon. Whether because of injury, change in strategy, or a play that needs to be made, you must be ready! Get your mind, body, and spirit in position when called upon to perform. Carry yourself in a way that your team knows that whatever is needed in the game today, if you are called upon you will be ready to *step up!*

NOTES

_____

_____

_____

_____

_____

_____

_____

_____

_____

_____

_____

_____

_____

_____

_____

_____

_____

_____

Esther 4: ¹⁴ For if you remain completely silent at this time, relief and deliverance will arise for the Jews from another place, but you and your father's house will perish. Yet who knows whether you have come to the kingdom for such a time as this?" NKJV

REVEREND DR. DELAND J. MYERS SR. PH.D.

19

BE STEADFAST

1 Corinthians 15: [58] *Therefore, my beloved brethren, be steadfast, immovable, always abounding in the work of the Lord, knowing that your labor is not in vain in the Lord. NKJV*

In the Book of 1 Corinthians, Paul is writing to the church in the city of Corinth which he founded on one of his missionary journeys. He has gotten word that the church was having some issues and his letter was written in the hopes of correcting some of these issues. In his letter, Paul was teaching them some of the basics of the faith and encouraging them to stay faithful to the Lord. The verse in 1 Corinthians 15:58 gives them a word of direction and encouragement to continue to grow as individuals and as a group of believers in Christ. The verse essentially says that they should stay steadfast or committed, not allow themselves to be moved from what they believe, and keep doing the ministry work that God had called them to do. Moreover, they needed to know that the work they were doing was not worthless and that there will be a reward for their efforts, e.g., blessings in this life and eternal life hereafter.

As you approach today's game, I believe this verse can give you direction and encouragement as you prepare. The first word is to be steadfast and committed. As you approach the game today stay committed to the goals of the team and what you had planned for at the beginning of the season. Regardless of what you are facing today, stay committed and "trust the process". The second word is to be immovable. Let nothing move you from your goals and game plan today. The inference in this word is that there may be situations and circumstances that will seek to move you from your goals including the amount of playing time you were expecting, calls by the officials, actions to provoke you by your opponent, and even when the score is not in your favor. You must not move from your commitment to the process. The final point is to keep working. Don't quit during the game and keep true to what your role is; no matter the score, the weather, officiating, what your opponent does, etc. Know that your efforts will have a benefit in reaching your team and personal goals.

I encourage all of you, individually and collectively as a team, to embrace these words in help you prepare and keep your focus on the game and your goals. Stay committed to the goals that you have agreed to; no matter what has happened in previous games or the challenge of today's opponent. Don't allow circumstances and situations to allow you to be moved from what you have committed yourself to; no matter what you face today. Finally, keep working, even if it looks like you are not making progress in the time and way that you thought. It may not look like it is having an effect but trust the process and know that all of your efforts are not in vain. *Be Steadfast!*

NOTES

1 Corinthians 15: [58] Therefore, my beloved brethren, be steadfast, immovable, always abounding in the work of the Lord, knowing that your labor is not in vain in the Lord. NKJV

20

SHAKE IT OFF

Acts 28: ³ But when Paul had gathered a bundle of sticks and laid them on the fire, a viper came out because of the heat, and fastened on his hand.... ⁵ But he shook off the creature into the fire and suffered no harm. NKJV

The Book of Acts gives the account of Paul and his companions after being shipwrecked on an island and trying to find a way to keep themselves warm. In the process of making the fire, a very poisonous and deadly snake attaches to Paul's hand. Everyone witnessing this expected the snake to kill Paul, he simply "shook it off" and continued to work on making the fire.

In life, there will be times when you are trying to move forward and do the things necessary in life to take of yourself, family, etc. and there will be things that will come up that are poisonous and deadly to you and your efforts. These "challenges" would destroy most people and in fact, those who know of your situation will expect you to "fall apart". But like Paul, as a believer, you do not have to become afraid or lose your confidence in what you are trying to do. Through the power of the Holy Spirit you can "shake it off" and keep doing what you need to do to be successful in life because you can do all things through Christ (Philippians 4:13). Please know that shaking it off does not mean the challenge is not there anymore or that it will be easy; shaking it off means that you are determined to not let this stand in your way and that you can overcome anything by the power of God's Spirit that lives within you.

In today's game there may be one or more 'situations" that would look to most fans, media, and even your opponent that you and your

REVEREND DR. DELAND J. MYERS SR. PH.D.

team cannot recover from, e.g., the loss of a teammate to injury, a turnover, a poor call by an official, a disagreement with a teammate or coach, and/or a score that looks insurmountable. Today, I challenge you that if one or more of these things happen you need to "shake it off" and keep moving forward toward your goals. As a believer, you should know that nothing is impossible to you and God has gifted you with your ability and His Spirit to never give up and not let situations or circumstances lose your focus. So today, be committed individually and as a team that whatever happens in today's game, no matter how insurmountable and/or difficult it looks, you are going to "shake it off" and keep playing to win. Know that you are more than a conqueror (Romans 8:37) against anything that you face. You will not be deterred or denied; keep playing to win and *shake it off!*

NOTES

_____
_____
_____
_____
_____
_____
_____
_____
_____
_____
_____
_____
_____
_____
_____
_____
_____
_____
_____
_____
_____
_____

Acts 28: ³ But when Paul had gathered a bundle of sticks and laid them on the fire, a viper came out because of the heat, and fastened on his hand.... ⁵ But he shook off the creature into the fire and suffered no harm. NKJV

REVEREND DR. DELAND J. MYERS SR. PH.D.

21

GROW UP

1 Corinthians 13: ¹¹ *When I was a child, I spoke as a child, I understood as a child, I thought as a child; but when I became a man, I put away childish things. NKJV*

In 1 Corinthians 13, Paul is speaking to the church at Corinth about how to live as believers and the key part of this chapter was to teach them to have love for one another and not be so consumed with the gifts that God had blessed them with. There were persons in the church who had been blessed with one or more tremendous gifts, including the gift to prophesy, heal, speak in different languages, etc. In fact, the gifts that they had been blessed with were to be used to serve each other. In that way, the church and the people who were a part of the church would be stronger. In verse 11 he says that being more concerned about themselves and getting their way was childish and when you mature/ grow up, you should put away such childish thinking.

This same concept applies to your team. All of you are blessed with tremendous gifts/abilities to play the sport that you compete in. Some those gifts include speed, strength, agility, etc. Some of you are blessed with more than one of these gifts and can perform them at an extremely high level. The same message that Paul had for the members of his team, e.g., The Church, applies to you and the members of your team also. To be a great team and play at a winning/championship level takes maturity and moving away from "childish" behavior. You need to be thinking not of only yourselves, but others on the team and how the gifts that you have been given can help the team win. That will mean that you may not be able to be the focal point of all of the plays, have to modify your playing style, and/or help to encourage other teammates when you are not in the game. If adversity comes and the direction of the game is not going your way, you cannot lose your composure and lose the ability to help your team win. Be mature in your actions and understanding. Be committed to keeping your emotions under control and directing your passions toward the team goals of winning the game and enhancing the gifts and abilities God has placed in you. By doing so, you will be a better player and more importantly, the entire team will benefit. Today, focus on using your gifts in a "grown-up" manner and by doing so, you and the team will *grow up!*

NOTES

_____
_____
_____
_____
_____
_____
_____
_____
_____
_____
_____
_____
_____
_____
_____
_____
_____
_____
_____
_____
_____

1 Corinthians 13: [11] When I was a child, I spoke as a child, I understood as a child, I thought as a child; but when I became a man, I put away childish things. NKJV

22

DON'T MOVE THE LANDMARK

Proverbs 22: ²⁸ Do not remove the ancient landmark Which your fathers have set. NKJV

The Book of Proverbs is a collection of God's wisdom in the scriptures that provides us with direction on how to live our lives so we can be successful in life. Proverbs 22:8 tells us not to move landmarks that those who have gone before us have set. The verse is referring to the ancient landmarks that were used to determine property lines and if the landmark was removed, the owners of the land could not determine whether they owned the land or not. This undoubtedly would lead to confusion and possibly the loss of land that you rightfully owned.

Looking at this verse more broadly, it means that you should not change the things that you were taught by your elders that were just, right, and in accordance with God's Word. If you do, your life will become confused and you are likely to lose those things that are rightfully yours that have been given by God including peace, joy, freedom, and material blessings God has for us.

The application for today's game is that you have been given the landmarks that your team stands for and are an important part of the culture of the team. These are landmarks that have been established by the coaches and former players that has resulted in a winning tradition. These landmarks could include discipline, toughness, strength, playing fast, fundamentals, unity, etc. Your opponent's goal today is to move you and your team away from those landmarks. They can do this through their game planning, attempts at intimidation, trash-talking, and even the band and their fans. If they are successful, you will become, lost, confused, and cause you to forget who you are as an individual player and team resulting in losing a game that you should be able to compete in and win.

Today, don't move your team landmarks. No matter what adversity you face, the score, calls by the officials that are not going your way, or even an injury to one of your players, you never forget what you stand for and how you plan to win. So, as you prepare for today's game, be determined to keep what has been established as the key elements of who you are as a team. Remember the game plan, prepare yourselves mentally, physically, and spiritually, and be determined that no matter what occurs in this game, *never move the landmarks* that have been established as the foundation of this team!

NOTES

Proverbs 22: [28] Do not remove the ancient landmark Which your fathers have set. NKJV

REVEREND DR. DELAND J. MYERS SR. PH.D.

23

BE CAREFUL YOU DON'T FALL

1 Corinthians 10: [12]*...let him who thinks he stands take heed lest he fall. NKJV*

In 1 Corinthians 10, Paul gives a summary of the story of the Children of Israel in the wilderness and how they had all the advantages of being God's chosen people but never reached the promised land because of their lack of faith in God, following their own lusts as opposed to focusing on God wanted and constantly complaining about what they didn't have as opposed to being grateful for what they did have. As a result, they never reached their goal of reaching the promised land and the blessings God had for them. Paul then tells us that this was written so we do not make the same mistakes found in 1 Corinthians 10:12 says that we should beware if we think this could not happen to us or we could fall and miss the blessings God has for us.

This message should be heeded by your team today. I am sure you know of teams who did not reach their full potential although they had all the elements of a winning team and yet did not reach their goals. Perhaps they lost their focus on the goals they had set, complained about what they didn't have as opposed to focusing on their own strengths and advantages they did have, and/or began looking at their own desires as opposed to what was best for the team. The danger in this is that we look at those teams and never learn from their mistakes and do the same things. Moreover, we see what happened to those teams and don't think this could happen to you and your team.

The same word that Paul had for them applies to you and your team as well. If you think this could not happen to you, you are doomed to make the same mistakes. As a team and as an individual player, don't think that you are immune to making the same errors in judgment. Make sure you have faith in your coaches and all the plans that have been established and agreed upon for this game today. Don't spend your time complaining about what is happening around you and look for solutions within your team and yourself.

Finally, don't get caught up in your wants and needs but those of the team. If you are not careful, you too will not meet all the goals that you are striving for due to thinking that you and your team are perfect and "have it all together". Be careful that you do not make the same mistakes and miss your opportunity to win this game today. Learn from the mistakes of others and stay focused so that you and your team do not fall.

NOTES

_____

_____

_____

_____

_____

_____

_____

_____

_____

_____

_____

_____

_____

_____

_____

_____

_____

_____

_____

_____

1 Corinthians 10: ¹²...let him who thinks he stands take heed lest he fall. NKJV

24

TAKE THE FIGHT TO YOUR OPPONENT

1 Samuel 17: [48] *So it was, when the Philistine arose and came and drew near to meet David, that David hurried and ran toward the army to meet the Philistine. NKJV*

The story of David's battle with Goliath is one of the most well-known passages of scripture found in the Bible. 1 Samuel 17 gives the account of the young man, David, who faced an opponent who was bigger, stronger, and more experienced in battle than he was.

David however, believed that he had been prepared to face Goliath although he did not have the size and experience of his opponent and ultimately beat Goliath on the field of battle.

One key aspect of this battle that many people overlook is how David approached Goliath before the battle which I believe was a key part of his victory. In 1 Samuel 17:48, the bible says that David hurried and ran to meet his opponent. I believe this is an indication that David showed no fear, was confident in his abilities, and believed God had prepared him to fight Goliath which would lead him to be victorious.

In today's game, you may be facing an opponent that many are saying you cannot compete against due to their size, skill, and experience. I would encourage you to learn from David how to approach your opponent. Like David, you must believe that you have been prepared for the battle, that you have the ability to compete and beat this opponent, and that you have no fear about who you are going to face. The best way to demonstrate this is to take the fight to your opponent. Do not hold back and wait for your opponent to implement their game plan on you,

you implement your game plan on them. You should look forward to this game and run onto the field with the confidence in the team and yourself, that your preparation, ability, and passion for the game will be more than adequate to compete against your opponent. Do not hold back!! Know that you have everything you need to compete. Moreover, as David did, trust God that he has prepared you to meet that challenge you have today and *take the fight to your opponent!*

NOTES

1 Samuel 17: [48] So it was, when the Philistine arose and came and drew near to meet David, that David hurried and ran toward the army to meet the Philistine. NKJV

25

DON'T GIVE UP

Galatians 6: *⁹ Let us not get tired of doing good, for we will reap at the proper time if we don't give up. CSB*

As believers, living in this world the way God has called us to live can be confusing uncomfortable, and difficult. There are times when we are misunderstood, slandered, and treated unfairly; sometimes we get this treatment for doing what God asks us to do. Yet, Galatians 6:9 tells us that we must not get tired in the face of all these challenges and continue to do what God asks us to do. The encouraging word in this scripture is the promise God gives us that if we continue to "do good", we will reap the blessings God has for us. Those blessings can be physical, mental, and spiritual. This promise has one caveat however, we cannot give up or quit. In our Christian walk, let us claim this promise by continuing to do what God calls us to do and claim the blessings he has for us.

Your coaches have prepared you for this game today. That preparation began at the beginning of fall camp which included practice, body development, and understanding the culture and goals of the team. You now also have a game plan specific for today's opponent based on the foundation the coaches established in fall training camp. During this game, there will be situations that will occur that will cause adversity that you and the team will have to face. There will be times when the official's calls will not go your way, the score is not in your favor, and/or injuries can take place. When adversity comes and things are not going your way, there will be the temptation to go away from the game plan and culture that you have been taught thinking that this will help you to win the game. This, however, is the wrong approach;

in fact, this is exactly what your opponent wants you to do. One thing that you must always remember, no matter how bad it looks, sounds, or feels, you cannot give up. Believe that things will begin to work in your favor if you don't quit. What Galatians 6:9 says in our Christian walk, the same applies to this game today. If you continue to do what you have been taught, you will reap the benefits of all your preparation and planning if you don't quit. Keep doing the "good things" that you have been prepared to do and look for the benefits to come forth and *never, ever quit!*

NOTES

Galatians 6: [9] *Let us not get tired of doing good, for we will reap at the proper time if we don't give up. CSB*

26

STAY UNIFIED

Philippians 2:² ...being like-minded, having the same love, being of one accord, of one mind. NKJV

The strongest force that any organization can have is to be unified. There are numerous scriptures in the bible that refer to the importance and the power of unity. As believers, we focus on being unified in the direction and power of God. Paul, in Philippians 2:2 talks to the church at Philippi and tells them how great the church is doing and to make sure that they continue down the path of success as a church they need to be unified. They need to be "like-minded", meaning to think the same way regarding what Jesus wants us to do. Secondly, they need to have the same love, the love for Jesus Christ that He has for us. Thirdly, they need to be on one accord, even when they all do not agree on the process, they agree to disagree and keep moving forward. Finally, they are of one mind, meaning they are moving all in the same direction in thoughts and actions.

As you prepare for the game today, keep in mind the power of unity as a team and what you can accomplish in the game today. One of the goals of the opponent is to get you to play as individuals and not as a team and thereby, ruin your game plan and ability to compete. As a team, I encourage you to consider the words of Paul as you consider unity on your team as you prepare for today's game. Be like-minded in the goals that the team has discussed and what needs to be accomplished today. Have a love for the game and your teammates to what is best for them and the team. Be on one accord by not having petty disputes that can cause dissension on the team and even in times of disagreement and things not going your way, agree that the team is greater than one individual. Finally, be of one mind, understanding that you approach every aspect of the game with the team mindset and not let an official's call, a trash-talking opponent, words spoken by fans, injuries, etc., take you away from your goal of winning this game today. Remember this, as a unified team, you will be able to compete at the highest level in this game today; as a unified team, your chance of competing in and winning this game greatly increases. Believe in the power of unity, believe in the team, and believe in the power to compete and win this game today. *Stay unified!*

NOTES

_____

_____

_____

_____

_____

_____

_____

_____

_____

_____

_____

_____

_____

_____

_____

_____

_____

_____

_____

_____

_____

_____

Philippians 2: ² …being like-minded, having the same love, being of one accord, of one mind. NKJV

REVEREND DR. DELAND J. MYERS SR. PH.D.

27

THE ONE THING THAT CAN STOP YOU

Hebrew 12: [1] *... let us strip off every weight that slows us down, especially the sin that so easily trips us up. And let us run with endurance....NLT*

The Bible tells us that the Christian life is like a race. There will be good days and bad days but the bible also encourages us to keep going and don't quit. The writer in Hebrews 12:1 says that there is a "cloud of witnesses (those who have given us a path to follow)" encouraging us to keep running with endurance. The writer says, however, in order to be successful when we run, is to remove anything that will slow us down, especially, "the sin" that easily trips us up. The writer is telling us that no matter how hard we are running if we do not address the "sin that easily trips us up" we will not be able to run properly. We all know what that sin is and be assured that the enemy has "film" on us and knows what that sin is also. The sin can be a bad habit, attitude, lack of self-control, selfishness, etc. that has always been a problem for us and must be addressed if we are going to run this Christian race victoriously.

In today's game, there are those who have been and will continue to cheer you on today. Those persons include fans, family members, and former players who have set the example for you to follow to be successful. They are encouraging you to play smart, passionate, and with the mindset to play the entire game with endurance for 60 minutes. You have been practicing all week, preparing your body, watching game film, and now have a game plan in place. As you prepare ask yourself individually and as a team this question, what is that one thing that limits you from being the best you can be that can prevent you from playing your best? I am sure you know what it is, your coaches know what it is and your opponent who has also been watching game film may know what it is also. The one thing could be your attitude/ego that can prevent you from playing as a team. Maybe it is your temper that if not controlled, an official's call or "trash talk" from your opponent can cause you to get a penalty or even disqualify you from the game. Perhaps it's a lack of focus or some aspect of your game that your coach has repeatedly told you about that you still have not addressed. If you are not careful, this "one thing" can hinder you and be used by your opponent to keep you and the team from competing at the highest level.

Be committed to addressing that "one thing" issue today by remembering and implementing the correction you have received, asking for help from your coaches and teammates, and praying for strength. Be confident that as you prepare for the game, you are better prepared to encounter whatever happens during the game knowing that you have covered all your bases and that you have an entire team, coaches, and fans supporting you to play at your best. Continue to get prepared, commit to playing the entire game, and not overlook that *one thing* that your opponent can use against you to have you play less than your best.

NOTES

_____

_____

_____

_____

_____

_____

_____

_____

_____

_____

_____

_____

_____

_____

_____

_____

_____

_____

_____

_____

_____

Hebrew 12: ¹ … let us strip off every weight that slows us down, especially the sin that so easily trips us up. And let us run with endurance….NLT

28

STIR IT UP

2 Timothy 1: [6] Therefore I remind you to stir up the gift of God which is in you....NKJV

Timothy was a young minister in Ephesus that had been chosen by Paul to lead the church that Paul had started. The scriptures found in 1st and 2nd Timothy tell us that he was having some difficulty leading the church as there were persons questioning him because he was young (1 Tim 4:12) and others who were spreading false doctrine. In 2 Timothy 1:7, it appears that Timothy is being faced with fear of the people that is causing him not to do the work of the ministry. In the first chapter of 2 Timothy, Paul sends words of encouragement and challenges Timothy to use what he has been taught by his mother, grandmother, and Paul himself that has prepared him for the ministry. Moreover, God has placed tremendous gifts in him to handle anything that he is going to face. In 2 Timothy 1:6, he tells Timothy to "stir up" the gift God has placed in him and lead the church that God has given him because he has a Spirit of Power, Love, and a Sound Mind to handle any issues that he is going to face.

In today's game, you have an opponent to play who presents you with a challenge. There will be those who tell you that you are not ready to face this opponent. There will be those who tell you that you do not have what it takes to take on this opponent and you should be concerned about what this opponent can do to you on the field. Let me remind you, as Paul reminded Timothy, that you indeed have what it takes. You have been taught by your trainers, strength coaches, and position coaches who have developed your mind and body for this game. You have had numerous practices, viewed the game film, and played in other games to more that prepare you for today's opponent. Moreover, you have gifts that God has placed in you, e.g., speed, strength, toughness, intelligence, etc. to play on the field with anyone. What has been placed in you is a spirit of power that gives you strength to overcome any adversity. You have a spirit of love for the game to play it with passion. Moreover, you have the love for the team and teammates to not put yourself before the goals of the team. You also have the spirit of a sound mind to know that everything may not go your way, but you will come together to overcome it; do not let your opponent dupe you into doing something that will cause a penalty or get you disqualified.

You are more than ready to face the challenges in this game today. Therefore, for all of you, individually and collectively as a team, it is time to leave all the talk and what people say behind you. Get ready to *"stir up"* the gifts that God has placed in you and compete to win this game today!

NOTES

2 Timothy 1: ⁶ *Therefore I remind you to stir up the gift of God which is in you….NKJV*

29

DON'T WASTE TIME

*John 9: ⁴ I must work the works of Him who sent Me while
it is day; the night is coming when no one can work. NKJV*

Time is a limiting factor for all of us. We all have a certain amount of time to complete any task that is given to us. We cannot control, manipulate or hold on to it. The Bible tells us that God is in control of all time. The Book of James (James 4:15) tells us that we must always keep this in mind by stating that "if the Lord wills" then we will do things we plan to do. Even the Lord Jesus during the time of His ministry clearly understood that there was a certain amount of time the Father gave him to do His work. He stated in John 9:4 that he had to do the works The Father sent Him to do because the time was coming when no person can work.

As you prepare for today's game, are you aware that you have only a certain amount of time to compete in this game? You have been prepared to compete in this game today by going through a week of practice, viewing the game film, training sessions, and meetings to prepare for this game. Today you will go through walk-throughs, team meetings, sessions with trainers, and the preparation on the field of competition right before the game. You must be aware, however, that you have only 60 minutes to bring all of this together to compete at the highest level. Both you and your opponent have only 60 minutes to compete. The team that best uses that time will be victorious.

Therefore, there will be no time to lose your focus on the game. You need to focus on the game at hand. You cannot be concerned with issues off the field; no time to spend time talking about issues that don't impact the game, no time if you have petty disagreements with your teammates, coaches, or your playing time/statistics. Everything you do now has to be focused on the game. Because when the 60 minutes is up and the referee calls the game, no one is going to be playing. You have a game to play and assignments/tasks appointed to you for this game. You have 60 minutes of game time to make it happen. The clock is ticking and the 60 minutes of game time will be over and you want to make sure that you made the most of it. Don't waste time team on worthless pursuits in preparation for this game. Don't waste very valuable time because when the time is over no one, including you, will be able to change it! *Don't waste time!*

NOTES

_____

_____

_____

_____

_____

_____

_____

_____

_____

_____

_____

_____

_____

_____

_____

_____

_____

_____

_____

_____

_____

John 9: ⁴ I must work the works of Him who sent Me while it is day; the night is coming when no one can work. NKJV

30

DON'T GET SIFTED

Luke 22: ³¹ And the Lord said, "Simon, Simon! Indeed, Satan has asked for you, that he may sift you as wheat. NKJV

Before the time when our Lord and Savior Jesus Christ would be tried, accused, beaten, and crucified for our sins he spoke to His disciples to prepare them for what was to come. The Book of Luke records (Luke 22:31) that Jesus then tells Simon Peter that the enemy had a plan to "sift him as wheat". Essentially what Jesus was telling Simon Peter was that the enemy wanted to manipulate him in such a way as to make Simon look bad and ruin his effectiveness as a witness for Jesus. In the next verses, however, Jesus tells him that he was praying for Simon that his faith would not fail and he would get through this difficult time; and when he gets through the test, Simon should strengthen his brothers (Luke 22:32-33). As believers, the enemy tries to ruin our witness for Jesus having us do or say something that we should not. We must remember during this time of testing to hold on to what must have faith in what Jesus has taught us. Unfortunately, the scriptures tell us that Simon Peter did not listen and the enemy caused him to fall as he denied knowing Jesus not once, or twice, but three times.

Today you have a very challenging game ahead of you. Your coaches have tried to prepare you all week for what you are going to face. You have worked with the trainers and strength coaches. You have worked with your position coach and head coach in meetings viewing game film. You have been practicing all week to implement the game plan that has been established. Your opponent's goal is to sift you, e.g., to make all that you have prepared during the week ineffective. Your opponent will do this through their own game plan after viewing game film on you and the team. They will use intimidation by how they approach you on the field and through "trash talk". They use their band, cheerleaders, and fans to get into your head so that you lose your focus on what you have been prepared to do. Please know, that the only way to get through this "sifting process" is to hold on to what you have been taught throughout the week. No matter what you hear, see, feel, or any other adversity you encounter, keep faith in all your preparations and do not lose focus. Moreover, if you see another teammate who is having trouble keeping their focus, please encourage them.

You have a great opportunity to do something special today on the field and you have been prepared. Your opponent knows this and will use every tactic they can to get you "off your game" by any means necessary. But keep praying and know that others are praying that you do not lose faith in yourself and what you have been taught. Finally, as you overcome things your opponent is trying to do, make sure to encourage those who are having difficulty. Don't be like Simon Peter and not listen; heed the wisdom given to you today. If you do, your opponent will not sift you and you will have all you need to compete and win this game today. *Don't get sifted!*

NOTES

_____

_____

_____

_____

_____

_____

_____

_____

_____

_____

_____

_____

_____

_____

_____

_____

_____

_____

_____

_____

Luke 22: ³¹ And the Lord said, "Simon, Simon! Indeed, Satan has asked for you, that he may sift you as wheat. NKJV

REVEREND DR. DELAND J. MYERS SR. PH.D.

31

WHAT DO YOU SEE?

1 Samuel 17: [25] *"Have you seen the giant?" the men asked….* [26] *David asked the soldiers standing nearby,…. Who is this pagan Philistine anyway, that he is allowed to defy the armies of the living God?" NLT*

The story of David and Goliath, one of the most well-known stories in the Bible, speaks of how David, a young man, defeated the great giant Goliath. Much is made about how he defeated Goliath; the slingshot he used, that he did not wear armor like the other soldiers, and used Goliath's sword to ultimately defeat him. I want to suggest to you that David defeating Goliath did not begin with any of those things but right at the beginning before he challenged Goliath. The scriptures in 1 Samuel 17 say that Goliath, who was a giant of a man, stood before the other soldiers and challenged them, they ran away in fear. They saw a giant that could not be defeated because he had defeated many soldiers before.

David, on the other hand, saw Goliath as any other soldier and in fact, questioned how Goliath could come and challenge them because they had God on their side. In fact, David saw himself as victorious and asked the question, what do I get when I win!! From that point, on David knew he could defeat Goliath and all of his preparations focused on that belief which ultimately defeated Goliath.

As you prepare for today's game, what do you see? Do you see your opponent as a giant? They may have a reputation through media reports that talk about how good they are and moreover, have a record of success to substantiate all that is said about them. Their stadium has the reputation of being a difficult place to play and that the fans are loud and will try to intimidate you. Let me encourage you not to use the eyes of the world but to use the eyes of God and how you have been prepared. The opponent you are going to face are football players just like you. They prepare for games just like you. They need the same nourishment and trainers just like you. Moreover, they have the same amount of time, number of players and are subject to the same rules of the game just like you. Do not focus on who they are, focus on who you are! Claim that you have been prepared better than they have. You have excellent players too. You and your teammates have been gifted by the same God as they have. You have excellent coaches, and trainers, and work harder to be more prepared than they are. This is not a new challenge. This is not the first stadium you have played in where the fans are boisterous, loud and use language to try to discourage you and lose your focus. You have been challenged before and come through. You too have a record of success and had to overcome adversity and come through victorious. There are no giants today! You have another opponent who presents a challenge and gives you an opportunity to compete at the highest level. You should see yourselves as a team ready for the challenge. Focus your eyes on yourself, your strengths know that you can win!! *What do you see?*

NOTES

_____

_____

_____

_____

_____

_____

_____

_____

_____

_____

_____

_____

_____

_____

_____

_____

_____

1 Samuel 17: ²⁵ "Have you seen the giant?" the men asked....²⁶ David asked the soldiers standing nearby,.... Who is this pagan Philistine anyway, that he is allowed to defy the armies of the living God?" NLT

32

WHAT ARE YOU WAITING FOR?

Joshua 18: ³ Then Joshua said to the children of Israel: "How long will you neglect to go and possess the land which the LORD God of your fathers has given you? NKJV

When the children of Israel were freed from slavery, God promised them that He had land that was prepared just for them and that He would provide everything they needed. They needed to have faith in Him and follow what He commanded them to do. The Bible tells us that unfortunately, they did not do what God said and stayed in the wilderness for 40 years under Moses. When Joshua became their leader, many of the people began to follow God's leadership and began to possess the land that God had promised them. Some tribes, however, still had not possessed the land God had promised them. In Joshua 18:3, Joshua shows his frustration with them and asks them what were they waiting for. Other tribes had taken possession of their land and God had given them the same resources that the others had. In the next verses, he told them to go to work!! He put together a plan for them to implement and take possession of those things God had promised them and stop waiting and making excuses and do what they were more than capable to do.

In today's game, you are being challenged to play like you are capable of playing. You have been blessed with everything you need to compete at the highest levels. You have knowledgeable trainers and strength coaches, experienced position coaches, workout facilities, practice facilities, meeting rooms, and game film. You as a team have been blessed with players who have been gifted with all the intelligence, speed, strength, agility, etc., necessary to compete at the highest levels. Unfortunately, to this point, you have not played to the level of the resources that you have.

Today's question is, what are you waiting for? I know that you have been faced with adversity, injuries, unfair/poor officiating, and some personal challenges during this year. However, other teams also face the same challenges and they have been playing at a higher level than you have. The time for excuses is over! It is time for you as a team to decide to play at the level that you can play at. The coaches have put together a game plan that will put you in position to win this game today!! You need to come together and execute the plan that has been put in place. Today is the day to take the steps necessary to reach the goals that have been set for this team. Do not let your opponent take what is yours today. You have the resources, you have the plan, and you have been prepared. Be the team you know you can be. *What are you waiting for?*

NOTES

Joshua 18: ³ Then Joshua said to the children of Israel: "How long will you neglect to go and possess the land which the LORD God of your fathers has given you? NKJV

33

DO YOU HAVE A MIND TO WORK?

Nehemiah 4: ⁶ So we built the wall....,for the people had a mind to work. NKJV

The Book of Nehemiah tells the story of a man, Nehemiah, who God called to rebuild the wall around the temple in Jerusalem that had been destroyed during the war 70 years earlier. He had many challenges ahead of him including getting resources and enemies who tried everything to prevent the wall from being built. Their enemies were used to being in control and the building of the wall threatened that control. Therefore, they did everything they could to prevent the wall from being built including discouragement, intimidation, and outright violence. The verse in Nehemiah 4:6 tells us the primary earthly reason why he and the people overcame these challenges and built the wall; realizing of course the power of God that was behind all of it. The primary reason was not the resources provided by the King of Persia, his assessment of the situation, or his intelligence in understanding how to build the wall. He states that all of those things would not have been enough if the people did not have a "mind to work". This means the people had decided in their mind that this plan was going to take a lot of effort and collectively agreed to put in the work to make it happen.

Throughout this year you have been building an organization to meet the goals established and agreed upon by the team. You have had to obtain resources, facilities, coaches, fan and family support, etc., to meet those goals. You have had challenges to overcome to allow you to continue to keep striving towards those goals. Today, you have an obstacle in front of you that seeks to derail you from the goals that you have set. Your opponent also has been working all year and has personal and team goals. Many of their goals are in conflict with yours including winning this game today. Moreover, they are ready to do whatever it takes to stop you from winning this game today.

Your goal, individually and collectively as a team today is to continue to work toward the goals that you have set. Moreover, you will plan to follow the game plan that has been set, given any modifications that will be necessary during the game. Finally, and most importantly, you understand that it will be difficult and you will face adversity today; however, you have the mind to put in the work necessary to overcome the challenges to win this game today.

This means no matter the weather, official calls, unfortunate injuries, "trash talking" from your opponent and their fans, or the score. You have the mind to work and win this game realizing that all of the hard work you have put in during the year, this past week, and today will enable you to overcome anything that you are going to face. So before, you take the field today, make a decision; do you have the mind to work and put in the effort necessary to win this game; or will you allow circumstances and situations to prevent you from being the victor today?

Do you have a mind to work?

NOTES

_____

_____

_____

_____

_____

_____

_____

_____

_____

_____

_____

_____

_____

_____

_____

_____

_____

_____

_____

_____

_____

Nehemiah 4: ⁶ So we built the wall….,for the people had a mind to work. NKJV

34

ARE YOU ALL IN?

Romans 12: ¹I beseech you …that you present your bodies a
living sacrifice, …, which is your reasonable service. ² And
do not be conformed to this world, but be transformed by the
renewing of your mind,…NKJV

In the Book of Romans, the Apostle Paul outlines much of the doctrine of Christianity to the believers in Rome. In Romans 7:14-25 he talks about how difficult this is in light of the sin that he battles in his life. In Romans 12: 1-2, Paul gives us the foundation of how we should live to be successful in today's world as a Christian. He first says that we have to give everything; body, mind, and spirit, e.g., our bodies. Moreover, in this life you will have to be sacrificial, meaning we will have to sacrifice some of our wants and desires to get there. He also says that this is the first necessary step (reasonable service) to being victorious. Then he says you can't keep the same mindset of the world, but be changed by having a new and different way to think. Then you will see the direction and power God will have in your life.

In today's contest, you have a major challenge ahead of you. The team that you face is determined to defeat you and everyone, experts and fans alike, do not believe that you have a chance to win or even compete in this game. We can use the model that the Apostle Paul gives us in Romans 12, to prepare for this opponent. The first thing is that you must decide that you are "all in". Everything that you are as a person and team member will be on display today. You must be ready to put it all "on the line" to compete in this game today.

You must continue to prepare yourself physically, mentally, and yes, spiritually to prepare for such a challenge. You must also be ready to do this sacrificially, meaning that it will cost you something. You have to put aside your wants and desires, off-the-field issues, and your own desires on the field such as how often you play, and how many touches of the ball you get. You will also have to "tolerate" some things that are said about you on the field for the good of the team. This will be the "first step" in competing against this opponent.

The second step is to not think about what everyone else is saying about the opponent you are going to face. This is going to take a "renewal" of your mind. You cannot think what everyone else thinks. You have the ability, preparation, coaching, and game plan necessary to compete and have this as your mindset when you approach this game today. If you do this, you will be able to enter the field and be ready to compete against this opponent and any adversity you are going to face. So today, do you want to compete? If so, are you all in? Are you ready to put all that you have into this game today? Are you ready to sacrifice and do want is necessary to compete against this opponent; yourself first and then as a member of this team? Are you ready to put aside what everyone is saying and change how you approach this game with the right mindset?

If so, then prepare to play and know that you are indeed ready to compete against this opponent and have every chance to win this game. *Are you all in?*

NOTES

_____

_____

_____

_____

_____

_____

_____

_____

_____

_____

_____

_____

_____

_____

_____

_____

_____

_____

_____

Romans 12: ¹I beseech you …that you present your bodies a living sacrifice, …, which is your reasonable service. ² And do not be conformed to this world, but be transformed by the renewing of your mind,…NKJV

REVEREND DR. DELAND J. MYERS SR. PH.D.

35

BUILT ON A ROCK

Matthew 7: [25] and the rain descended, the floods came, and the winds blew and beat on that house; and it did not fall, for it was founded on the rock. NKJV

In the famous "Sermon on the Mount" found in Matthew 5-7, Jesus provided those listening at that time and us today, with words that inform us about the basics of the Christian faith. These include key concepts including: 1) we are the salt of the earth and light of the world; 2) the importance of helping those in need; 3) the importance of prayer; and 4) the importance of priorities and the dangers of judging others. Jesus ends His message by saying if you live according to His teaching, you will be like a house built on a rock. He says in Matthew 7:25 that storms will come and no matter how they beat on the house, it would not fall. On the other hand, if you don't follow His teaching, the same storms will come but the house will not stand because it is built on sand, e.g., something that is not solid. Jesus is saying that no matter what you face in life, if you believe and hold fast to His teaching, nothing in life can stop you.

As you approach this game today, you must believe that everything you have worked toward as a member of this team from spring and fall practice, and the game planning for this week has been designed to put you and your teammates on a foundation that will stand no matter what you face today. Like the two houses that Jesus talks about in the "Sermon on the Mount", both teams today, you and your opponent will be faced with adversity. These could include the score, the weather, calls by the officials, and unfortunate injuries. The team that can withstand these challenges will be the team who will perform the best and come out victorious. You have put in the work, taken care of your bodies, prepared your minds, and adhered to the foundation that this team is built on. You have already overcome so much to get to this point today. If you continue to believe in everything you have been taught, believe in your coaches, your teammates, and the game plan, and know that there is nothing that will happen in this game that can deter you from competing at the highest level. What you have been built on is solid, time-tested, and will get you through any circumstance or what the opponent comes against you with. You have been built on a solid rock; a strong foundation and a culture that can win. Don't fall back, become anxious, or get flustered. There is nothing that can deter you; play at the highest levels; *you have been built on a rock!*

NOTES

Matthew 7: ²⁵ and the rain descended, the floods came, and the winds blew and beat on that house; and it did not fall, for it was founded on the rock. NKJV

36

GET OUT OF YOUR COMFORT ZONE

Luke 5: ⁴....He said to Simon, "Launch out into the deep and let down your nets for a catch." ⁵ But Simon answered and said to Him, "Master, we have toiled all night and caught nothing; nevertheless at Your word I will let down the net." NKJV

In Luke 5 Jesus had been teaching the people about how God would want them to live and to have faith. He had been teaching from the lake using a boat that Simon Peter and the others, who were experienced fishermen, had been using to catch fish. They had been fishing all night and had not caught anything. Jesus then implores him to go deeper in the water to catch the fish they wanted. Simon replies in verse 5 that he was an experienced fisherman, had been fishing all night, and nothing they had tried worked; but he trusted Jesus and did what he asked. The result was they had a tremendous catch of fish; more than they could handle. The lesson here was that trusting in Jesus and doing something out of the ordinary or your comfort zone can get you tremendous results.

Today you are going to face a tremendous challenge. The opponent you are facing is very tough. In fact, some of you have faced this opponent or others like them, and the results have not been good. Today your coaches are asking you to trust in the game plan and what you have been practicing and it will lead you to compete with this team. The plan may be one that asks you to get out of your comfort zone as part of the original game plan or after an adjustment to the game plan. In your mind, you don't view this plan as unworkable. You and your teammates may tell yourselves that you don't see how this is going to work. We tried this before and did not work; moreover, we ran this play before and could not execute it. In fact, we did not do very well in practice with these plays.

Today if you are being called upon to go "into the deep" and do something that you are not used to or accustomed to, you must trust the process. All of your planning efforts have got you this far and will carry you through this contest. If you want to compete against a team such as this, you are going to have to be unconventional and uncomfortable. Trust the plan that is in place. Stay focused and don't complain. Trust that your coaches know what is best and trust in the skills and gifts God has given you; and look for a tremendous result. If you and the team are called upon to go into the deep and be unconventional, trust the plan and go to compete and win this game today!

NOTES

Luke 5: ⁴ ....He said to Simon, "Launch out into the deep and let down your nets for a catch." ⁵ But Simon answered and said to Him, "Master, we have toiled all night and caught nothing; nevertheless at Your word I will let down the net." NKJV

37

A WINNING FORMULA

2 Timothy 4:⁷ I have fought a good fight, I have finished my course, I have kept the faith: KJV

The Apostle Paul is one of the models of faith for us as believers. Although he wrote 25 percent of the New Testament, Paul was not a perfect person.

He did not start out as a believer and in fact, persecuted those who were. When he became a believer, he talked about the struggles he had with sin (Romans 7:15-20), the persecution he encountered as a believer (2 Corinthians 11:25), and the trials he had when God did not answer his prayer and he had to depend on God's grace to overcome a major trial in his life (2 Corinthians 12:7-9). Despite all these challenges, at the end of his life, Paul said he was successful as a believer in Christ. One of the secrets of his success is found in 2 Timothy 4:7. He first said that he never gave up fighting; no matter what he faced. The second thing he says is that he finished HIS course. He did what God told him to do and he finished what he was supposed to do. He didn't try to do what he was not asked to do and never quit. Finally, he says that he kept the faith in Jesus despite the trials that could have caused him to quit or walk away. In 2 Timothy 4:8, Paul says because he did those aforementioned 3 things, he was a winner and God would crown him as a winner.

As you approach today's game, your goal, individually and collectively as a team, is to win. As you approach this game you will have challenges that you will face, some you can anticipate and others that you do not expect. I believe you can embrace the words of Paul for this game.

The first is that you don't stop fighting. Never let the opponent take the fight to win out of you. No matter what the score, how the officials are calling the game, weather conditions, etc., you must never stop fighting. Secondly, complete what your coach and game plan have asked you to do, and finish the game plan! On every play, every quarter, every half, the entire game. You can encourage others to do what they have been asked to do but you must make sure you are doing what you have been asked to do; there are no big or small responsibilities. Everyone must do their job and finish them. Finally, keep faith in yourself, the game plan, your coaches, and your teammates. Do not let your opponent cause you to lose faith in what you are doing and what you have been taught. If that happens, you will lose your confidence and take you out of position to win this game. If you do these three things today, I believe that you, like Paul, will be in position to compete and win this game!! Keep fighting, carry out and complete your job, and do not lose faith in the game plan, your teammates, or yourself. *This is a winning formula!*

NOTES

2 Timothy 4: [7] _I have fought a good fight, I have finished my course, I have kept the faith: KJV_

38

KEEP YOUR FOCUS

Matthew 14: ²⁹ "…So Peter went over the side of the boat and walked on the water toward Jesus. ³⁰ But when he saw the strong wind and the waves, he was terrified and began to sink. NLT

The biblical account of Peter walking on the water in Matthew 14:22-31 is one of the most well-known accounts in all of scripture. When someone is capable of doing something special, they say that the person can "walk on water". The key aspect of this account, however, is sometimes forgotten and/or misunderstood. While traveling in a boat, a storm arose and the disciples were having trouble navigating the boat in the storm. Jesus, knowing they were having difficulty sailing in the storm came out to be with them by walking on the water. The disciples became terrified thinking Jesus was a ghost; however, Peter seeing that it was Jesus asked if he too could walk on the water. When Jesus complied, Peter came out to Jesus walking on the water; however, when he took his eyes off Jesus and looked at the challenge of the storm, he began to sink. The takeaway message is that if we take our eyes off Jesus and focus on the problems, we will have difficulty and lose our faith.

The application of this message for today's game is to make sure that you are focusing on those things that brought you to this point and not on any difficulties or challenges that may face today. As you play this game today, the "storms" of competition can arise. You can get behind on the scoreboard, the fans, and your opponent can try to "rattle" you with the words they use, injuries could occur, "unkind" officiating and the weather could all come into play. If you begin to focus on these things, you can lose your focus on the game plan, your teammates, the direction your coaches are giving you, and/or the gifts God has blessed you with. This can result in the "sinking" of your ability to compete and win this game. When these "storms" of the game occur, you need to make sure you are focused on those things that will keep you "afloat" and have you in position to win the game. This can take a great amount of effort as adversity can indeed cause you to forget those things that can bring you success. No matter what it sounds like, looks like, or even feels like, keep your focus on the things that put you and keep you in a position to win. Keep focusing on the game plan, your training, your coaches, and playing within your ability. Don't look at the storm; keep focused and win! *Do not lose your focus today!*

NOTES

_____

_____

_____

_____

_____

_____

_____

_____

_____

_____

_____

_____

_____

_____

_____

_____

_____

_____

_____

_____

Matthew 14: ²⁹ "…So Peter went over the side of the boat and walked on the water toward Jesus. ³⁰ But when he saw the strong wind and the waves, he was terrified and began to sink. NLT

REVEREND DR. DELAND J. MYERS SR. PH.D.

39

WHOSE PRAISE ARE YOU LOOKING FOR?

John 12: ⁴² Many people did believe in him, however, including some of the Jewish leaders. But they wouldn't admit it..... ⁴³ For they loved human praise more than the praise of God. NLT

Jesus had been performing miracles and teaching in the churches and to the people. The way he taught and the miracles He performed convinced many people that He was indeed the Messiah sent by God. John 12:42-43 tells us, although the evidence was clear to many of them, they refused to acknowledge Him as God's Messiah because they were more concerned about pleasing people than pleasing God. They were more concerned about how they looked to their friends, their family, or to persons who they thought could put them in positions of power and authority. As a result, they never got the opportunity to see and experience the blessings of Jesus. They never saw or appreciated his teachings, his miracles, and most of all, the salvation that Jesus gives to us all through his sacrifice on the cross.

There have been athletes and teams who have missed the blessings of winning and competing at the highest levels because they were concerned about what people thought of them. They were more concerned about how they looked in the uniform, more than making sure the equipment fits properly and would help them compete at the highest levels and keep them free from injury. They were more concerned about the dance they would do after they scored than making sure they were executing the plays they were given to be able to score. They were more concerned about how they looked after making a play on the field than getting ready for the next upcoming play. As a result, they were not focused, the team suffered, they did not compete at the highest levels, and missed the opportunity to win the game and reach team goals.

Whose praise are you looking for today? Praise from the crowd or praise from your coaches for playing the game properly and competing at the highest level. Don't get caught up in the hype! Focus on knowing and executing the game plan, and not losing your focus that could result in a costly mistake, penalty, or even disqualification. Look for praise from the coaches and leaders of the team and not the crowd and people you are trying to impress. Whose praise are you looking for?

NOTES

_____

_____

_____

_____

_____

_____

_____

_____

_____

_____

_____

_____

_____

_____

_____

_____

_____

_____

_____

_____

_____

John 12: ⁴² Many people did believe in him, however, including some of the Jewish leaders. But they wouldn't admit it….. ⁴³ For they loved human praise more than the praise of God. NLT

40

STAND

Ephesians 6: ¹³ Therefore take up the whole armor of God, that you may be able to withstand in the evil day, and having done all, to stand. ¹⁴ Stand therefore,....NKJV

As believers, we are told by the Apostle Paul in Ephesians 6 that to battle our enemy, we must be prepared. Paul tells us in verse 13 that we have to have the whole armor of God to be successful. He lists all the different parts of the armor, e.g., shield, helmet, breastplate, shoes, etc., and the purpose of each part of the armor to fight against the "wiles or tricks" of the enemy. Moreover, in verses 13 and 14, he says that you will be able to withstand anything that comes against you, and if you have done everything you can to stand, then stand. Do not fall back, become passive, or lose your confidence because you have something firm to stand on. Paul says by doing this we have confidence in living for Christ and being victorious in life.

As you prepare for the game today, have you done everything you to compete against your opponent? Have you learned the game plan that is going to be implemented? Have you practiced the plays that the coaching staff has covered with you all week during practice? Have you been diligent in the weight room and with the trainers to get your body prepared to play? Have you got sufficient rest and consumed the correct and right amounts of foods and beverages? If you have done these things, you should have nothing to be concerned about; stand on what you have done. No matter who your opponent is, no matter what the experts say, no matter what happens during the game with officiating, weather, or some unforeseen challenge, you can stand confidently on what you have done. There is no need to be anxious, worried, or concerned. Keep your focus and play the game the right way. Stand on your ability. Stand on your game preparations. Stand as a team committed to competing at the highest level. Stand tall as you enter this competition. You have done all to stand; so go and compete to win. *Stand!*

NOTES

Ephesians 6: [13] Therefore take up the whole armor of God, that you may be able to withstand in the evil day, and having done all, to stand. [14] Stand therefore,…NKJV

REVEREND DR. DELAND J. MYERS SR. PH.D.

Printed in the United States
by Baker & Taylor Publisher Services